MENSA
NUMBER
PUZZLES

THIS IS A CARLTON BOOK

Text & puzzle copyright © British Mensa Limited 1993
Design and artwork copyright © Carlton Books
Limited 1999

This Edition published by Carlton Books Limited 1999

A CIP catalogue for this book is available from the
British Library

ISBN 1 85868 309 2

Printed and bound in Great Britain

MENSA
NUMBER
PUZZLES

Harold Gale

CARLTON

AMERICAN MENSA

American Mensa Ltd is an organization for people who have one common trait: an IQ in the top 2% of the nation. Over 50,000 current members have found out how smart they are. This leaves room for an additional 4.5 million members in America alone. You may be one of them.

If you enjoy mental exercise, you'll find lots of good "workout programs" in the *Mensa Bulletin,* our national magazine. Voice your opinion in one of the newsletters published by each of our 150 local chapters. Learn from the many books and publications that are available to you as a member.

Are you a "people person," or would you like to meet other people with whom you feel comfortable? Then come to our local meetings, parties, and get-togethers. Participate in our lectures and debates. Attend our regional events and national gatherings. There's something happening on the Mensa calendar almost daily. So, you have lots of opportunities to meet people, exchange ideas, and make interesting new friends. Maybe you're looking for others who share your special interest? Whether yours is as common as crossword puzzles or as esoteric as Egyptology, there's a Mensa Special Interest Group (SIG) for it.

Take the challenge. Find out how smart you really are. Contact American Mensa Ltd today and ask for a free brochure. We enjoy adding new members and ideas to our high-IQ organization.

American Mensa Ltd,
1229 Corporate Drive West,
Arlington, TX 76006-6103.

Or, if you don't live in the USA and you'd like more details, you can contact Mensa International, 15 The Ivories, 628 Northampton Street, London N1 2NY, England, who will be happy to put you in touch with your own national Mensa.

INTRODUCTION

Puzzles using numbers have become more and more popular over the years. Some of the puzzles are purely mathematical and involve the use of simple processes. There are others, however, which, although appearing to use one branch of mathematics, can be solved more easily and quickly by using a little logical thought. Before attempting a puzzle it should be considered very carefully and suddenly you'll find that quite often the solution stands out clearly.

Harold Gale always insisted that credit should go to his extremely able helpers in putting this book together. Carolyn Skitt checked, criticized and improved on many of the puzzles produced. Without her help, this book might have still been in the making. Help also came from other quarters. Bobby Raikhy worked on the many diagrammatic styles you'll find within these pages, and puzzler David Ballheimer checked the proofs and made sure that everything worked.

All in all, I know you'll be pleased with the results.

Robert Allen,
Editorial Director,
Mensa Publications.

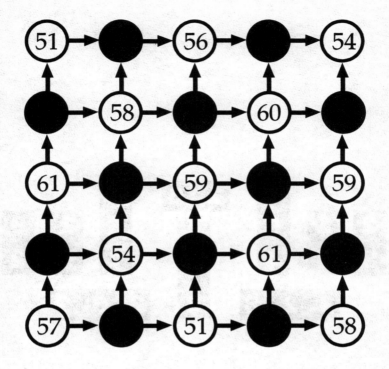

NUMBER PUZZLE 1

Move from the bottom left-hand corner to
the top right-hand corner following the arrows.
Add the numbers on your route together.
If each black spot is worth minus 23, how many
different routes are there to score 188?

ANSWER 62

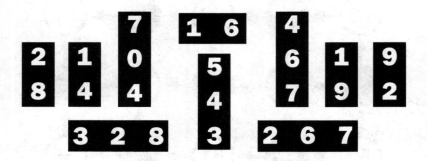

NUMBER PUZZLE 2

Place the tiles in a square to give some five-figure numbers. When this has been done accurately the same five numbers can be read both down and across. How does the finished square look?

ANSWER 10

NUMBER PUZZLE 3

Start in the middle circle and move from circle to touching circle. Collect the four numbers which will total 70. Once a route has been found return to the middle circle and start again.

If a route can be found, which obeys the above rules but follows both a clockwise and an anticlockwise path, it is treated as two different routes.

How many different ways are there?

ANSWER 103

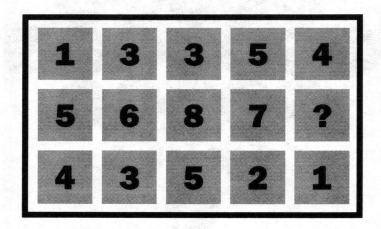

NUMBER PUZZLE 4

Which number should replace the question mark in
the diagram?

ANSWER 51

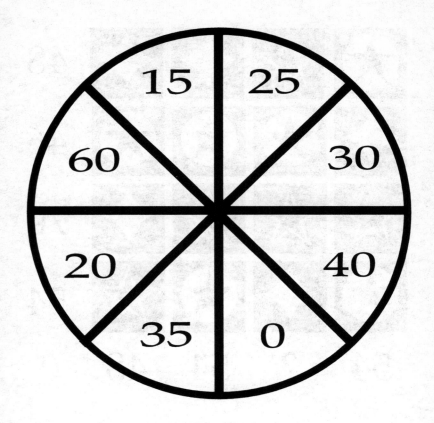

NUMBER PUZZLE 5

You have four shots with each go to score 75.
Aim at this target and work out how many
different ways there are to make the score. Assume
each shot scores and once four numbers have been
used the same four cannot be used again in
another order.
How many are there?

ANSWER 92

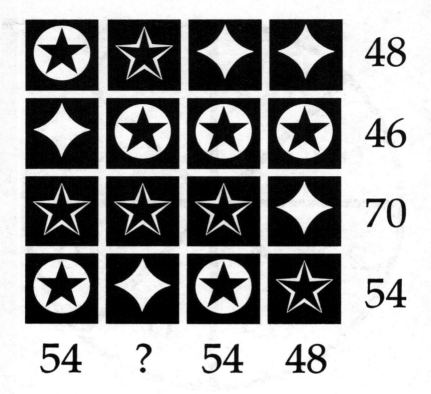

48

46

70

54

54   ?   54   48

NUMBER PUZZLE 6

The contents of each box has a value. The total of
the values is shown alongside a row or beneath a
column. Which number should replace the
question mark?

ANSWER 40

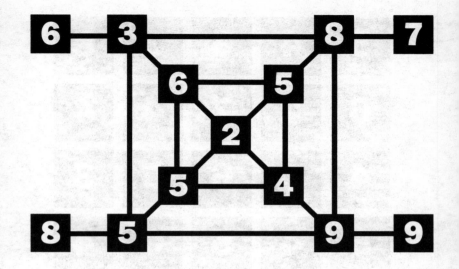

NUMBER PUZZLE 7

Start at any corner number and collect another four
numbers by following the paths shown. Add the
five numbers together.
What is the highest total which can be attained?

ANSWER 82

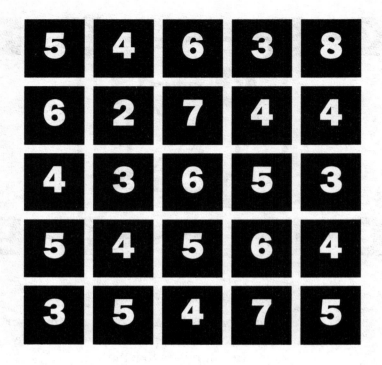

NUMBER PUZZLE 8

Move from square to adjacent square either
vertically or horizontally. Begin at the bottom
left-hand square and end at the top right-hand
square. Collect nine numbers and total them.
How many different ways are there to total 38?

ANSWER 30

A B C D E

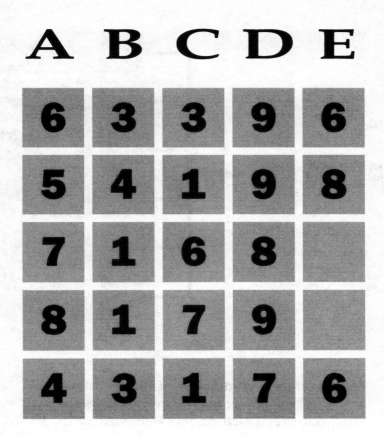

NUMBER PUZZLE 9

There is a relationship between the columns of numbers in this diagram. The letters above the grid are there to help you. Which number should be placed in the empty squares?

ANSWER 72

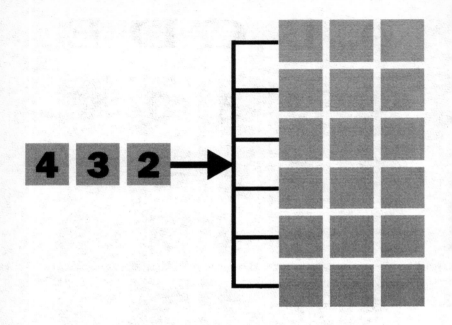

NUMBER PUZZLE 10

Place six three digit numbers of 100 plus at the end
of 432 so that six numbers of six digits are
produced. When each number is divided by 151 six
whole numbers can be found.
Which numbers should be placed in the grid?

ANSWER 20

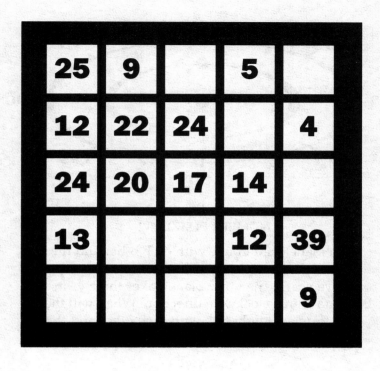

NUMBER PUZZLE 11

Each row, column and five-figure diagonal line
in this diagram must total 85. Four different
numbers must be used, as many times as necessary,
to achieve this.
What are the numbers?

ANSWER 61

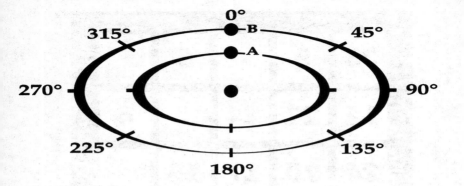

NUMBER PUZZLE 12

Two planets are in line with each other and the sun. The outer planet will orbit the sun every twelve years. The inner planet takes three years. Both move in a clockwise direction. When will they next form a straight line with each other and the sun? The diagram should help you.

ANSWER 9

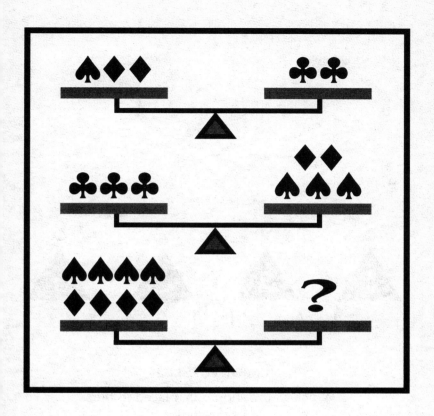

NUMBER PUZZLE 13

The top two scales are in perfect balance.
How many clubs will be needed to balance the
bottom set?

ANSWER 102

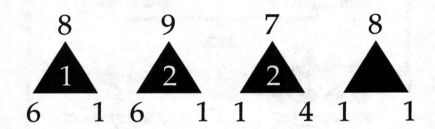

8
1
6 1

9
2
6 1

7
2
1 4

8
1 1

NUMBER PUZZLE 14

Which figure should be placed in the
empty triangle?

ANSWER 50

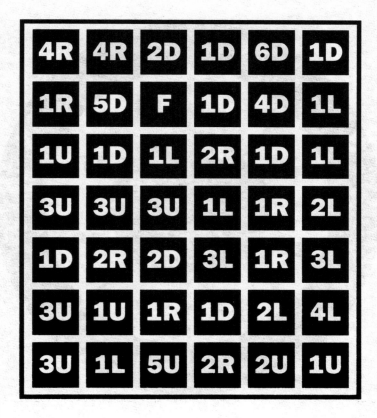

4R	4R	2D	1D	6D	1D
1R	5D	F	1D	4D	1L
1U	1D	1L	2R	1D	1L
3U	3U	3U	1L	1R	2L
1D	2R	2D	3L	1R	3L
3U	1U	1R	1D	2L	4L
3U	1L	5U	2R	2U	1U

NUMBER PUZZLE 15

Here is an unusual safe. Each of the buttons must
be pressed once only in the correct order to open it.
The last button is always marked F. The number of
moves and the direction is marked on each button.
Thus 1U would mean one move up
whilst 1L would mean one move to the left.
Which button is the first you must press.

ANSWER 91

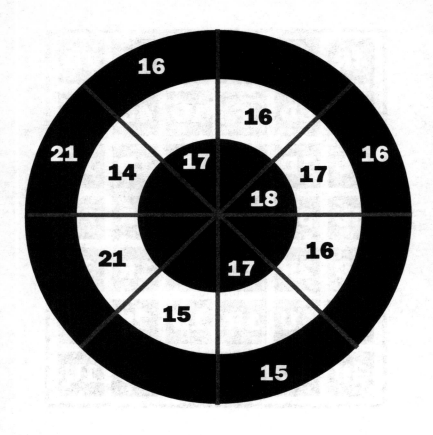

NUMBER PUZZLE 16

Complete the grid in such a way that each segment
of three numbers totals the same.
When this has been done correctly each of the three
concentric circles of eight numbers will produce
three identical totals.
Now complete the diagram.

ANSWER 39

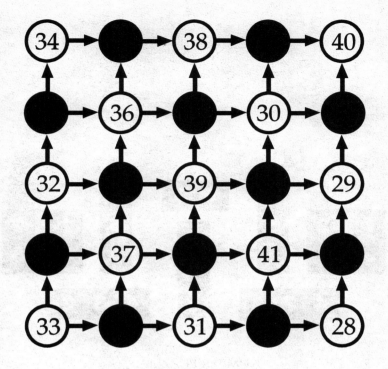

NUMBER PUZZLE 17

Move from the bottom left-hand corner to the top right-hand corner following the arrows. Add the numbers on your route together. If each black spot is worth minus 8, how many different routes are there to score 155?

ANSWER 81

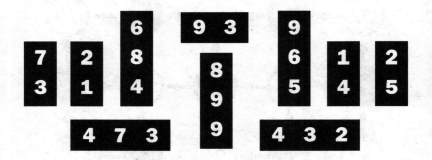

NUMBER PUZZLE 18

Place the tiles in a square to give some five-figure
numbers. When this has been done accurately the
same five numbers can be read both down and
across. How does the finished square look?

ANSWER 29

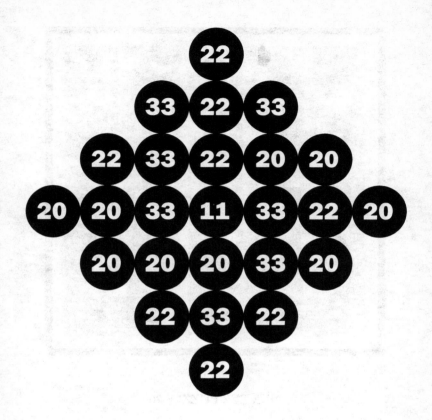

NUMBER PUZZLE 19

Start in the middle circle and move from circle to touching circle. Collect the four numbers which will total 86. Once a route has been found return to the middle circle and start again.

If a route can be found, which obeys the above rules but follows both a clockwise and an anti-clockwise path, it is treated as two different routes. How many different ways are there?

ANSWER 71

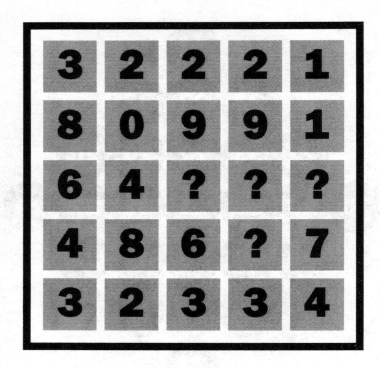

NUMBER PUZZLE 20

Which number should replace the question marks
in the diagram?

ANSWER 19

NUMBER PUZZLE 21

You have four shots with each go to score 51. Aim
at this target and work out how many different
ways there are to make the score. Assume each
shot scores and once four numbers have been used
the same four cannot be used again in another
order. How many are there?

ANSWER 8

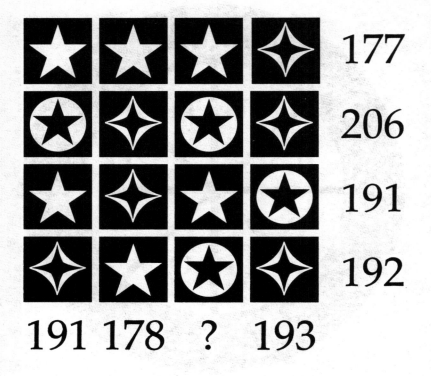

191 178 ? 193

NUMBER PUZZLE 22

The contents of each box has a value. The total of the values is shown alongside a row or beneath a column. Which number should replace the question mark?

ANSWER 60

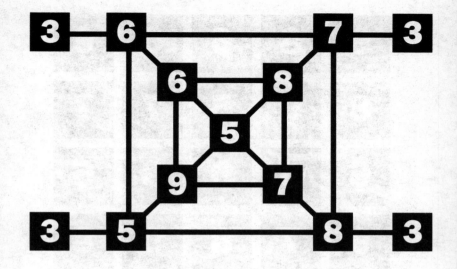

NUMBER PUZZLE 23

Start at any corner number and collect another four
numbers by following the paths shown. Add the
five numbers together.
How many times can you score 27?

ANSWER 101

NUMBER PUZZLE 24

Move from square to adjacent square either
vertically or horizontally. Begin at the bottom
left-hand square and end at the top right-hand
square. Collect nine numbers and total them. How
many different ways are there to total 66?

ANSWER 49

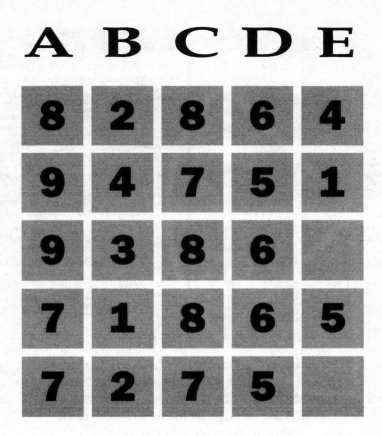

A	B	C	D	E
8	2	8	6	4
9	4	7	5	1
9	3	8	6	
7	1	8	6	5
7	2	7	5	

NUMBER PUZZLE 25

There is a relationship between the columns of
numbers in this diagram. The letters above the grid
are there to help you. Which number should be
placed in the empty squares?

ANSWER 90

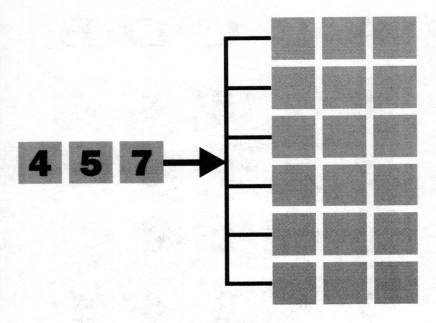

NUMBER PUZZLE 26

Place six three digit numbers of 100 plus at the end
of 457 so that six numbers of six digits are
produced. When each number is divided by 55.5
six whole numbers can be found. Which numbers
should be placed in the grid?

ANSWER 38

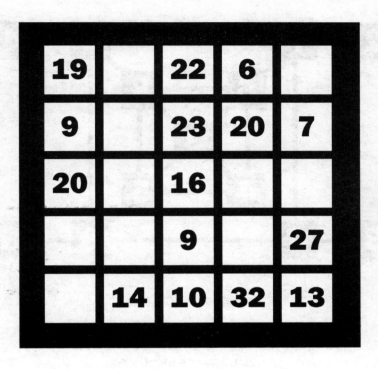

19		22	6	
9		23	20	7
20		16		
		9		27
	14	10	32	13

NUMBER PUZZLE 27

Each row, column and five-figure diagonal line in this diagram must total 80. Three different numbers must be used, as many times as necessary, to achieve this.
What are the numbers?

ANSWER 80

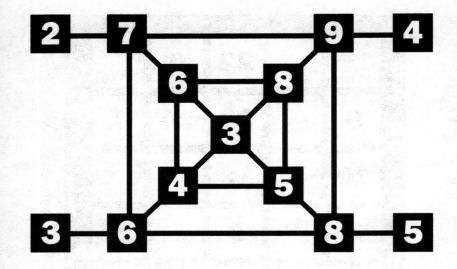

NUMBER PUZZLE 28

Start at the corner number and collect another four
numbers by following the paths shown. Add the
five numbers together.
How many times can you score 24?

ANSWER 28

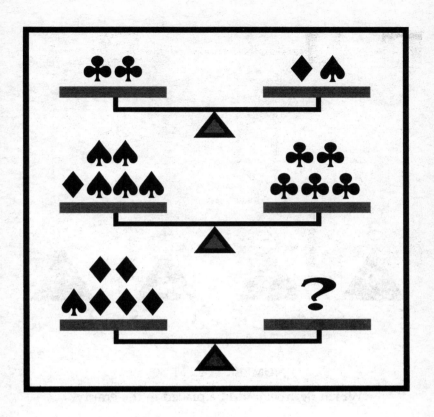

NUMBER PUZZLE 29

The top two scales are in perfect balance.
How many clubs will be needed to balance the
bottom set?

ANSWER 70

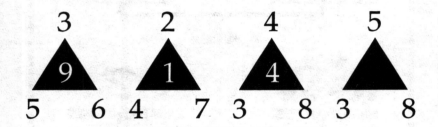

NUMBER PUZZLE 30

Which figure should be placed in the empty
triangle?

ANSWER 18

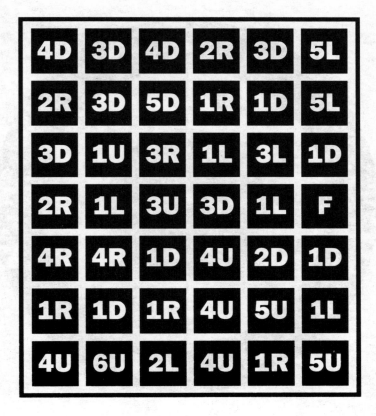

4D	3D	4D	2R	3D	5L
2R	3D	5D	1R	1D	5L
3D	1U	3R	1L	3L	1D
2R	1L	3U	3D	1L	F
4R	4R	1D	4U	2D	1D
1R	1D	1R	4U	5U	1L
4U	6U	2L	4U	1R	5U

NUMBER PUZZLE 31

Here is an unusual safe. Each of the buttons must
be pressed once only in the correct order to open it.
The last button is always marked F. The number of
moves and the direction is marked on each button.
Thus 1U would mean one move up whilst 1L
would mean one move to the left.
Which button is the first you must press?

ANSWER 59

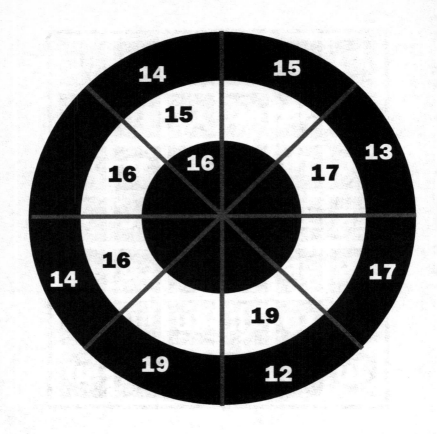

NUMBER PUZZLE 32

Complete the grid in such a way that each segment
of three numbers totals the same.
When this has been done correctly each of the three
concentric circles of eight numbers will produce
three identical totals.
Now complete the diagram.

ANSWER 7

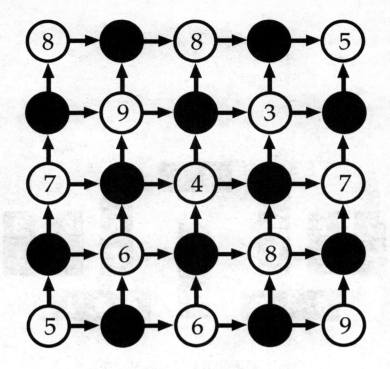

NUMBER PUZZLE 33

Move from the bottom left-hand corner to the top right-hand corner following the arrows. Add the numbers on your route together. If each black spot is worth 2, how many different routes are there to score 40?

ANSWER 100

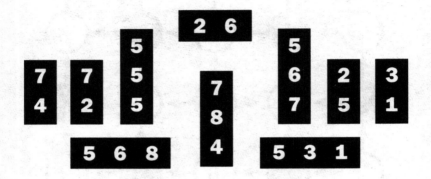

NUMBER PUZZLE 34

Place the tiles in a square to give some five-figure numbers. When this has been done accurately the same five numbers can be read both down and across. How does the finished square look?

ANSWER 48

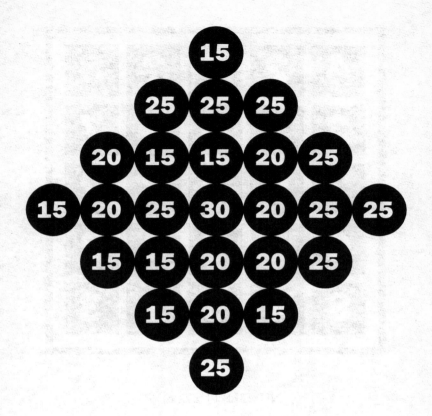

NUMBER PUZZLE 35

Start in the middle circle and move from circle to touching circle. Collect the four numbers which will total 90. Once a route has been found return to the middle circle and start again.

If a route can be found, which obeys the above rules but follows both a clockwise and an anticlockwise path, it is treated as two different routes. How many different ways are there?

ANSWER 89

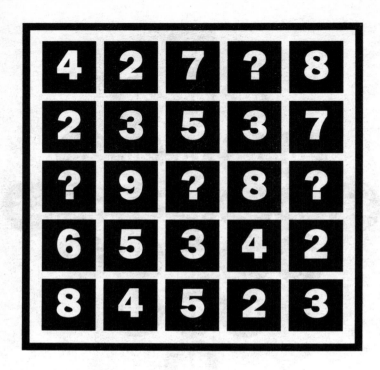

NUMBER PUZZLE 36

Which number should replace the question mark in
the diagram?

ANSWER 37

NUMBER PUZZLE 37

You have four shots with each go to score 49.
Aim at this target and work out how many
different ways there are to make the score. Assume
each shot scores and once four numbers have been
used the same four cannot be used again in
another order. How many are there?

ANSWER 79

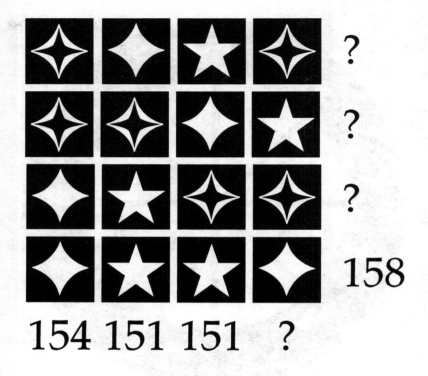

154 151 151 ?

NUMBER PUZZLE 38

The contents of each box has a value. The total of the values is shown alongside a row or beneath a column. Which number should replace the question marks?

ANSWER 27

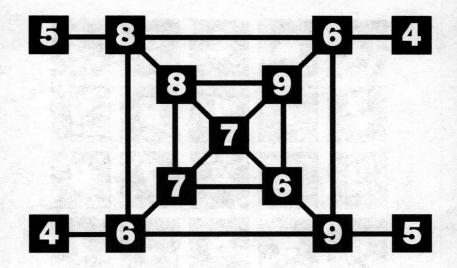

NUMBER PUZZLE 39

Start at the corner number and collect another four
numbers by following the paths shown. Add the
five numbers together.
What is the lowest number you can score?

ANSWER 69

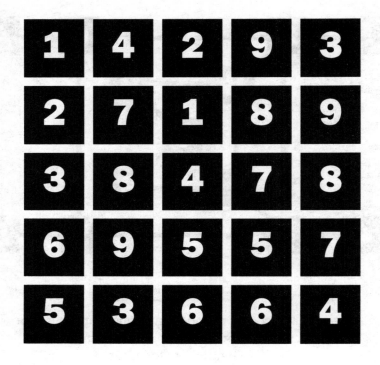

NUMBER PUZZLE 40

Move from square to adjacent square either
vertically or horizontally. Begin at the bottom
left-hand square and end at the top right-hand
square. Collect nine numbers and total them.
How many different ways are there to total 35?

ANSWER 17

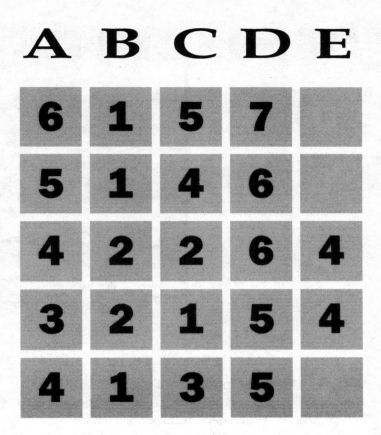

NUMBER PUZZLE 41

There is a relationship between the columns of numbers in this diagram. The letters above the grid are there to help you. Which number should be placed in the empty squares?

ANSWER 58

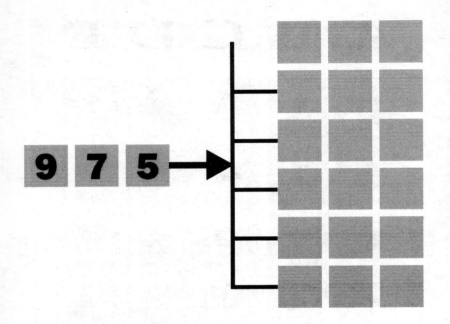

NUMBER PUZZLE 42

Place six three digit numbers of 100 plus at the end
of 975 so that six numbers of six digits are
produced. When each number is divided by
65.5 six whole numbers can be found. Which
numbers should be placed in the grid?

ANSWER 6

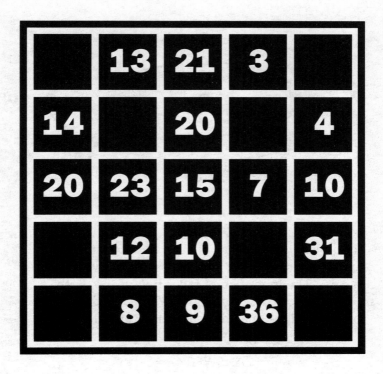

NUMBER PUZZLE 43

Each row, column and five-figure diagonal line
in this diagram must total 75. Three different
numbers must be used, as many times as necessary,
to achieve this.
What are the numbers?

ANSWER 99

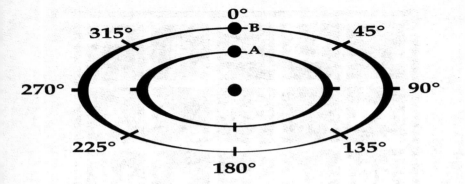

NUMBER PUZZLE 44

Two planets are in line with each other and the
sun. The outer planet will orbit the sun every six
years. The inner planet takes two years. Both
move in a clockwise direction. When will they next
form a straight line with each other and the sun?
The diagram should help you.

ANSWER 47

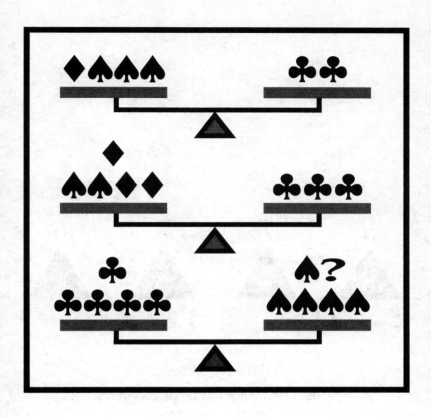

NUMBER PUZZLE 45

The top two scales are in perfect balance.
How many diamonds will be needed to balance the
bottom set?

ANSWER 88

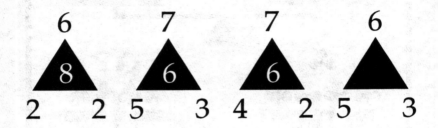

NUMBER PUZZLE 46

Which figure should be placed in the
empty triangle?

ANSWER 36

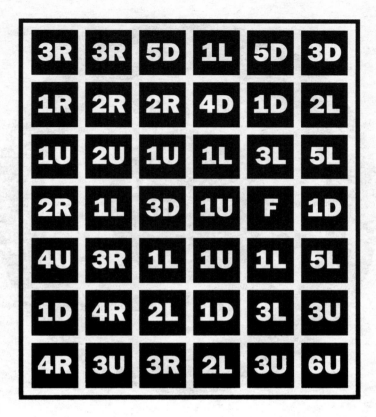

NUMBER PUZZLE 47

Here is an unusual safe. Each of the buttons bar
one must be pressed once only in the correct order
to open it. The last button is always marked F.
The number of moves and the direction is marked
on each button. Thus 1U would mean one move up
whilst 1L would mean one move to the left.
Which button is the first you must press?

ANSWER 78

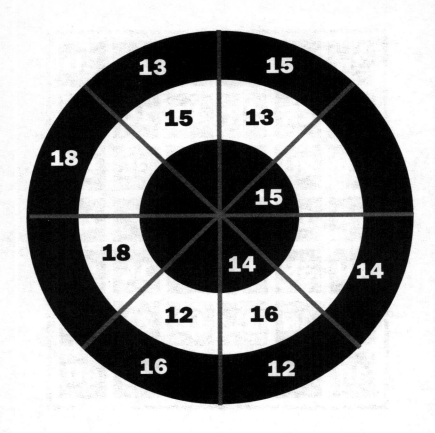

NUMBER PUZZLE 48

Complete the grid in such a way that each segment
of three numbers totals the same.
When this has been done correctly each of the three
concentric circles of eight numbers will produce
identical totals.
Now complete the diagram.

ANSWER 26

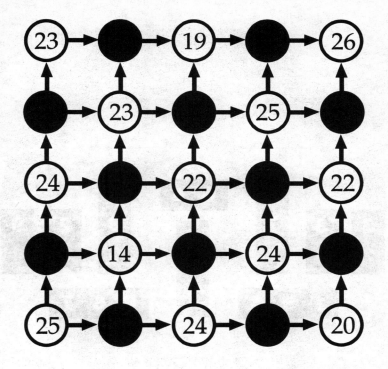

NUMBER PUZZLE 49

Move from the bottom left-hand corner to the top right-hand corner following the arrows. Add the numbers on your route together. If each black spot is worth minus 13, how many different routes are there to score 69?

ANSWER 68

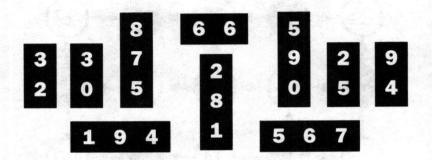

NUMBER PUZZLE 50

Place the tiles in a square to give some five-figure numbers. When this has been done accurately the same five numbers can be read both down and across. How does the finished square look?

ANSWER 16

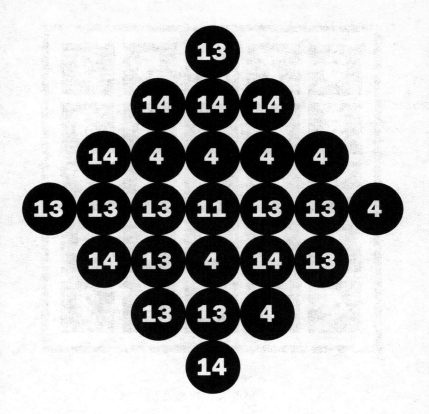

NUMBER PUZZLE 51

Start in the middle circle and move from circle to touching circle. Collect the four numbers which will total 42. Once a route has been found return to the middle circle and start again.
If a route can be found, which obeys the above rules but follows both a clockwise and an anticlockwise path, it is treated as two different routes. How many different ways are there?

ANSWER 57

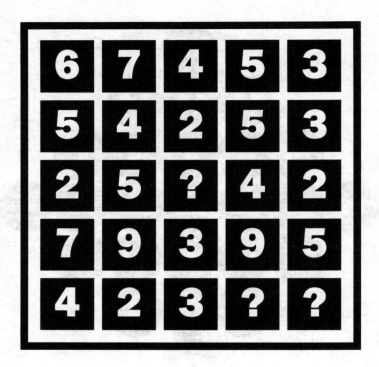

NUMBER PUZZLE 52

Which number should replace the question marks
in the diagram?

ANSWER 5

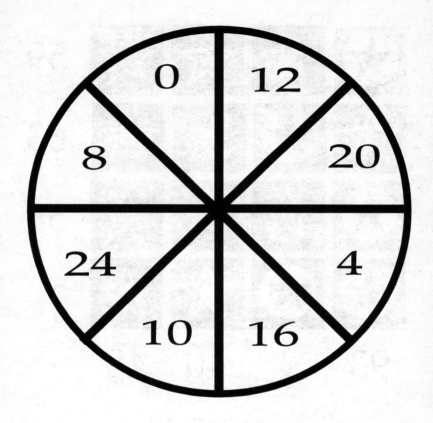

NUMBER PUZZLE 53

You have four shots with each go to score 48. Aim
at this target and work out how many different
ways there are to make the score. Assume each
shot scores and once four numbers have been used
the same four cannot be used again in another
order. How many are there?

ANSWER 98

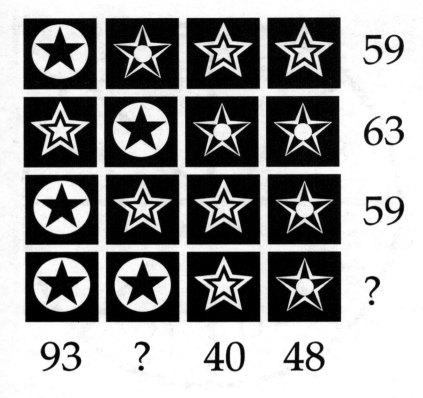

NUMBER PUZZLE 54

The contents of each box has a value. The total of the values is shown alongside a row or beneath a column. Which number should replace the question marks?

ANSWER 46

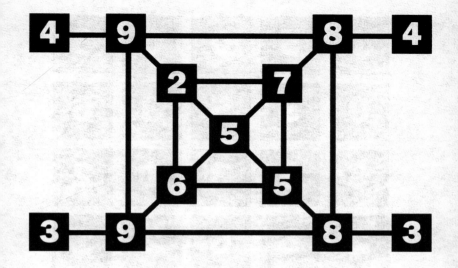

NUMBER PUZZLE 55

Start at any corner number and collect another four
numbers by following the paths shown. Add the
five numbers together.
How many times can you score 29?

ANSWER 87

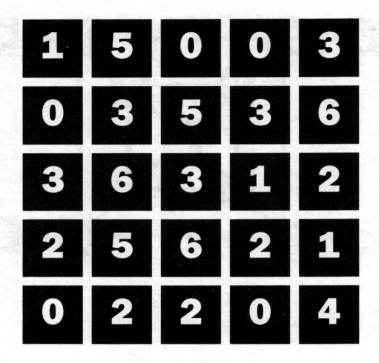

NUMBER PUZZLE 56

Move from square to adjacent square either
vertically or horizontally. Begin at the bottom
left-hand square and end at the top right-hand
square. Collect nine numbers and total them.
How many different ways are there to total 30?

ANSWER 35

A B C D E

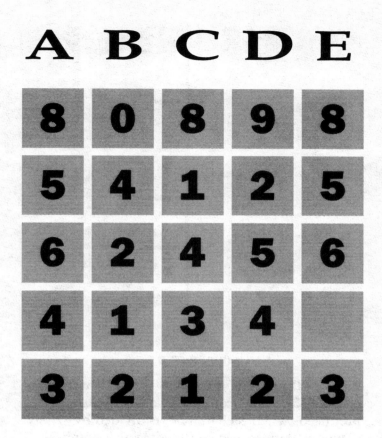

A	B	C	D	E
8	0	8	9	8
5	4	1	2	5
6	2	4	5	6
4	1	3	4	
3	2	1	2	3

NUMBER PUZZLE 57

There is a relationship between the columns of
numbers in this diagram. The letters above the grid
are there to help you. Which number should be
placed in the empty squares?

ANSWER 77

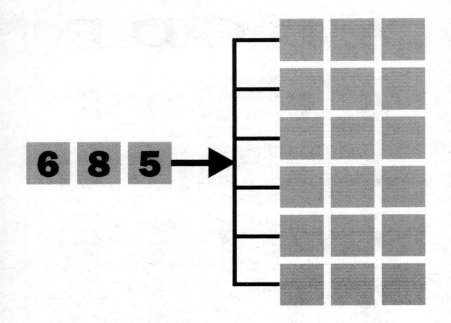

NUMBER PUZZLE 58

Place six three digit numbers of 100 plus at the end of 685 so that six numbers of six digits are produced. When each number is divided by 111 six whole numbers can be found. Which numbers should be placed in the grid?

ANSWER 25

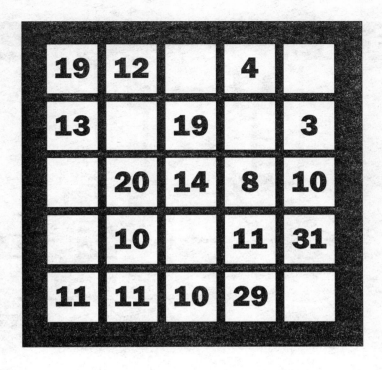

NUMBER PUZZLE 59

Each row, column and five-figure diagonal line
in this diagram must total 70. Three different
numbers must be used, as many times as necessary,
to achieve this.
What are the numbers?

ANSWER 67

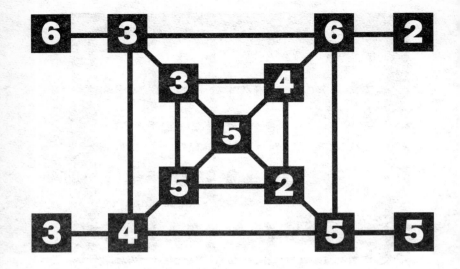

NUMBER PUZZLE 60

Start at the corner number and collect another four
numbers by following the paths shown. Add the
five numbers together.
How many times can you score 17?

ANSWER 15

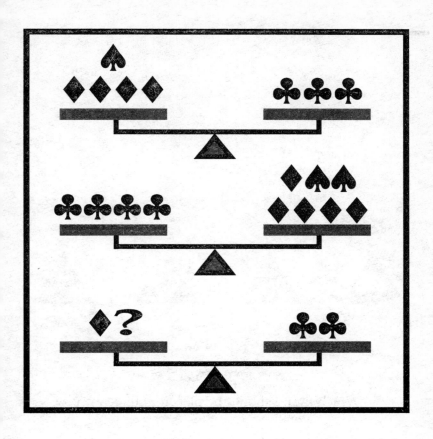

NUMBER PUZZLE 61

The top two scales are in perfect balance.
How many spades will be needed to balance the
bottom set?

ANSWER 56

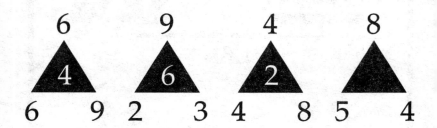

NUMBER PUZZLE 62

Which figure should be placed in the empty triangle?

ANSWER 4

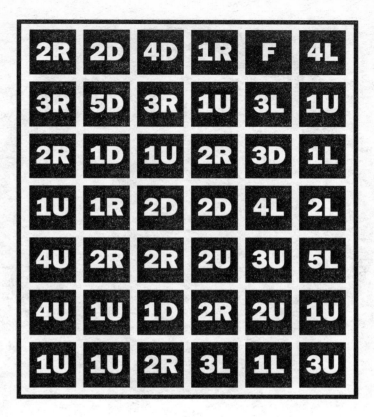

2R	2D	4D	1R	F	4L
3R	5D	3R	1U	3L	1U
2R	1D	1U	2R	3D	1L
1U	1R	2D	2D	4L	2L
4U	2R	2R	2U	3U	5L
4U	1U	1D	2R	2U	1U
1U	1U	2R	3L	1L	3U

NUMBER PUZZLE 63

Here is an unusual safe. Each of the buttons must
be pressed once only in the correct order to open it.
The last button is always marked F. The number of
moves and the direction is marked on each button.
Thus 1U would mean one move up
whilst 1L would mean one move to the left.
Which button is the first you must press?

ANSWER 97

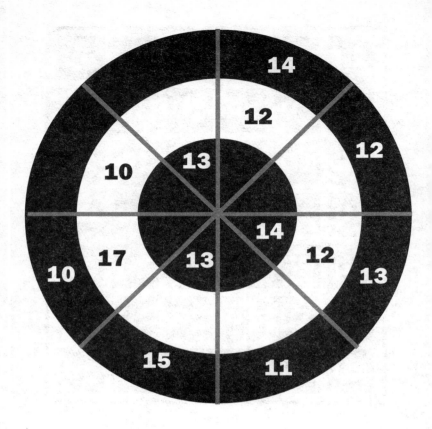

NUMBER PUZZLE 64

Complete the grid in such a way that each segment
of three numbers totals the same.
When this has been done correctly each of the three
concentric circles of eight numbers will produce
identical totals.
Now complete the diagram.

ANSWER 45

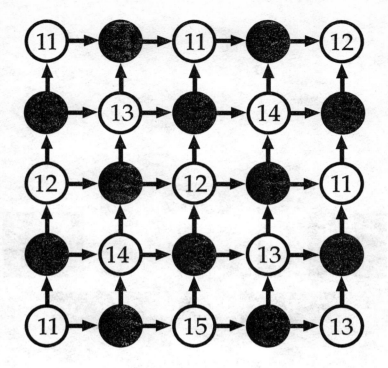

NUMBER PUZZLE 65

Move from the bottom left-hand corner to the top right-hand corner following the arrows. Add the numbers on your route together. If each black spot is worth 9, how many different routes are there to score 94?

ANSWER 86

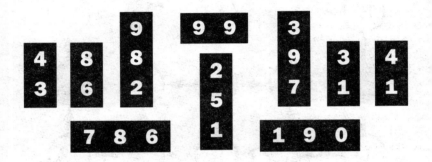

NUMBER PUZZLE 66

Place the tiles in a square to give some five-figure
numbers. When this has been done accurately the
same five numbers can be read both downwards
and across. How does the finished square look?

ANSWER 34

NUMBER PUZZLE 67

Start in the middle circle and move from circle to touching circle. Collect the four numbers which will total 15. Once a route has been found return to the middle circle and start again.
If a route can be found, which obeys the above rules but follows both a clockwise and an anticlockwise path, it is treated as two different routes. How many different ways are there?

ANSWER 76

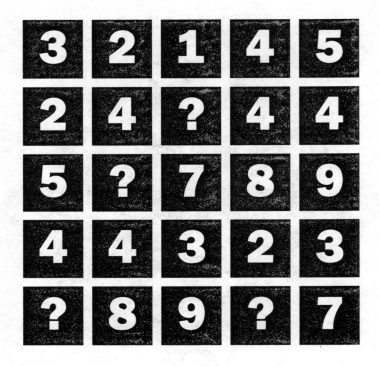

NUMBER PUZZLE 68

Which number should replace the question marks
in the diagram?

ANSWER 24

NUMBER PUZZLE 69

You have three shots with each go to score 26. Aim
at this target and work out how many different
ways there are to make the score. Assume each
shot scores and once three numbers have been used
the same three cannot be used again in another
order. How many are there?

ANSWER 66

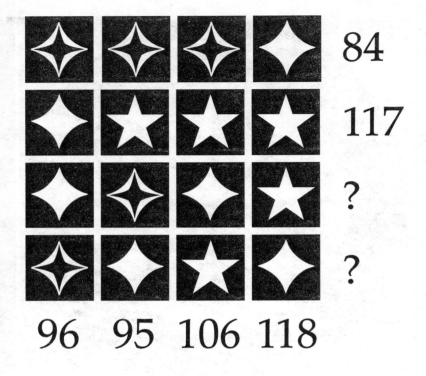

84

117

?

?

96 95 106 118

NUMBER PUZZLE 70

The contents of each box has a value. The total of
the values is shown alongside a row or beneath a
column. Which number should replace the
question marks?

ANSWER 14

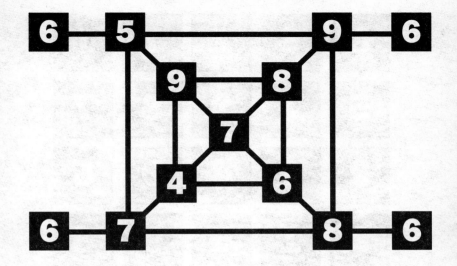

NUMBER PUZZLE 71

Start at any corner number and collect another four
numbers by following the paths shown. Add the
five numbers together.
What is the highest number you can score?

ANSWER 55

NUMBER PUZZLE 72

Move from square to adjacent square either
vertically or horizontally. Begin at the bottom
left-hand square and end at the top right-hand
square. Collect nine numbers and total them.
What is the lowest possible score?

ANSWER 3

A B C D E

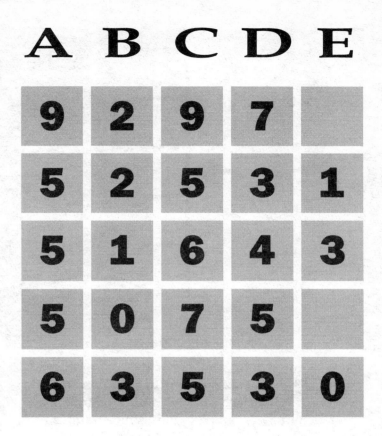

A	B	C	D	E
9	2	9	7	
5	2	5	3	1
5	1	6	4	3
5	0	7	5	
6	3	5	3	0

NUMBER PUZZLE 73

There is a relationship between the columns of
numbers in this diagram. The letters above the grid
are there to help you. Which number should be
placed in the empty squares?

ANSWER 96

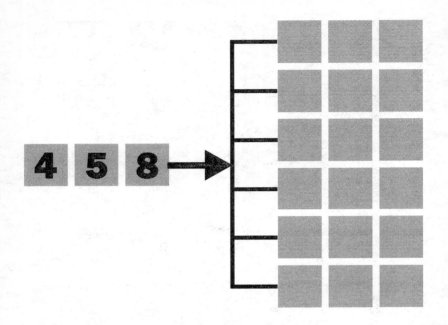

NUMBER PUZZLE 74

Place six three digit numbers of 100 plus at the end
of 458 so that six numbers of six digits are
produced. When each number is divided by 122 six
whole numbers can be found. Which numbers
should be placed in the grid?

ANSWER 44

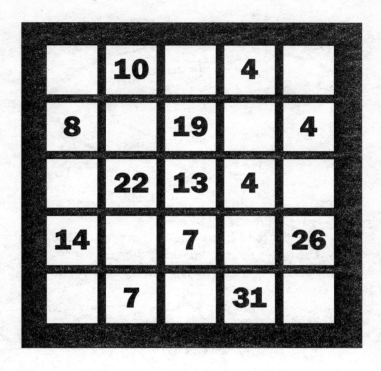

	10		4	
8		19		4
	22	13	4	
14		7		26
	7		31	

NUMBER PUZZLE 75

Each row, column and five-figure diagonal line
in this diagram must total 65. Two different
numbers must be used, as many times as necessary,
to achieve this.
What are the numbers?

ANSWER 85

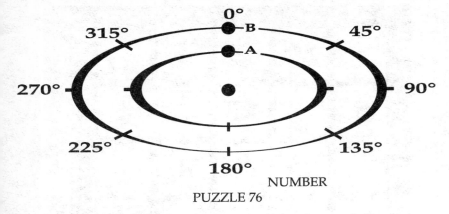

NUMBER

PUZZLE 76

Two planets are in line with each other and the sun. The outer planet will orbit the sun every fifteen years. The inner planet takes five years. Both move in a clockwise direction. When will they next form a straight line with each other and the sun? The diagram should help you.

ANSWER 33

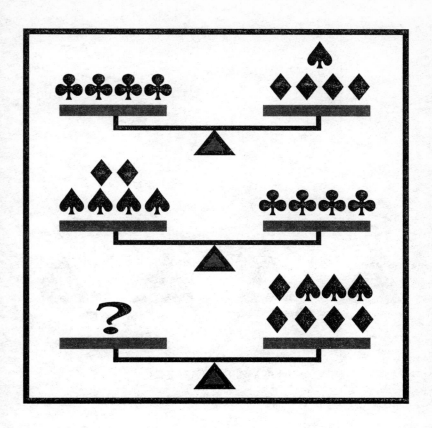

NUMBER PUZZLE 77

The top two scales are in perfect balance.
How many clubs will be needed to balance the
bottom set?

ANSWER 75

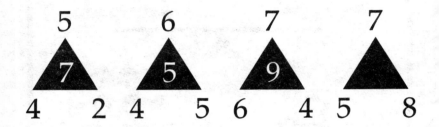

NUMBER PUZZLE 78

Which figure should be placed in the empty triangle?

ANSWER 23

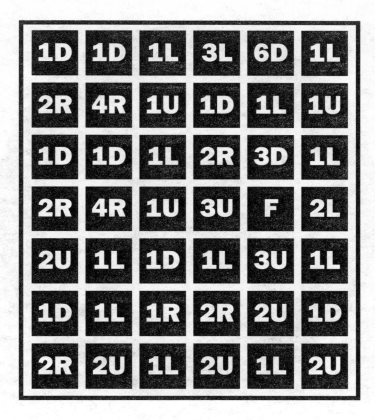

1D	1D	1L	3L	6D	1L
2R	4R	1U	1D	1L	1U
1D	1D	1L	2R	3D	1L
2R	4R	1U	3U	F	2L
2U	1L	1D	1L	3U	1L
1D	1L	1R	2R	2U	1D
2R	2U	1L	2U	1L	2U

NUMBER PUZZLE 79

Here is an unusual safe. Each of the buttons must
be pressed once only in the correct order to open it.
The last button is always marked F. The number of
moves and the direction is marked on each button.
Thus 1U would mean one move up
whilst 1L would mean one move to the left.
Which button is the first you must press?

ANSWER 65

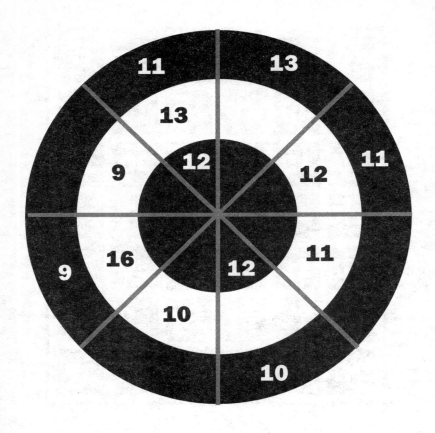

NUMBER PUZZLE 80

Complete the grid in such a way that each segment
of three numbers totals the same.
When this has been done correctly each of the three
concentric circles of eight numbers will produce
identical totals.
Now complete the diagram.

ANSWER 13

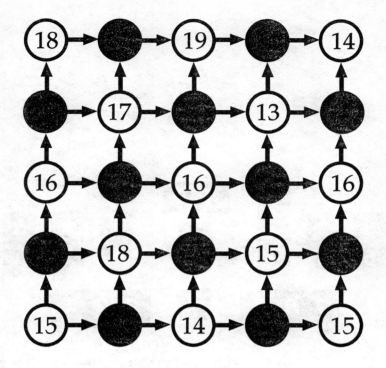

NUMBER PUZZLE 81

Move from the bottom left-hand corner to the top
right-hand corner following the arrows. Add the
numbers on your route together. If each black spot
is worth minus 7, how many different routes are
there to score 51?

ANSWER 54

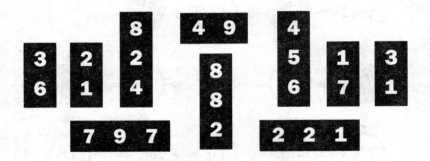

NUMBER PUZZLE 82

Place the tiles in the square to give some five-figure numbers. When this has been done accurately the same five numbers can be read both down and across. How does the finished square look?

ANSWER 2

NUMBER PUZZLE 83

Start in the middle circle and move from circle to touching circle. Collect the four numbers which will total 100. Once a route has been found return to the middle circle and start again.
If a route can be found, which obeys the above rules but follows both a clockwise and an anticlockwise path, it is treated as two different routes. How many different ways are there?

ANSWER 95

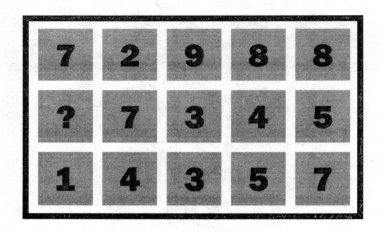

NUMBER PUZZLE 84

Which number should replace the question mark in
the diagram?

ANSWER 43

NUMBER PUZZLE 85

You have three shots with each go to score 42. Aim at this target and work out how many different ways there are to make the score. Assume each shot scores and once three numbers have been used the same three cannot be used again in another order. How many are there?

ANSWER 84

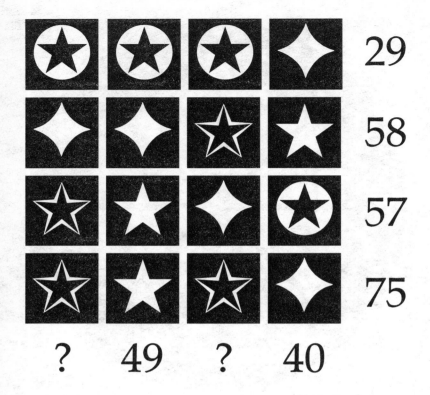

29

58

57

75

?   49   ?   40

NUMBER PUZZLE 86

The contents of each box has a value. The total of the values is shown alongside a row or beneath a column. Which number should replace the question mark?

ANSWER 32

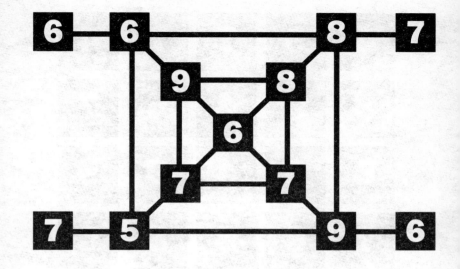

NUMBER PUZZLE 87

Start at any corner number and collect another four
numbers by following the paths shown. Add the
five numbers together.
What is the highest number you can score
and how many times can you score it?

ANSWER 74

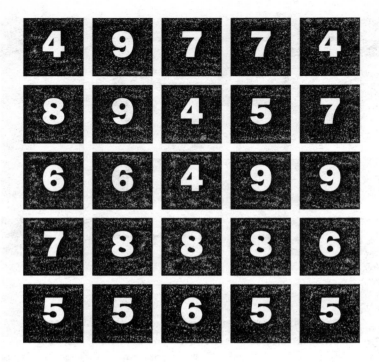

NUMBER PUZZLE 88

Move from square to adjacent square either
vertically or horizontally. Begin at the bottom
left-hand square and end at the top right-hand
square. Collect nine numbers and total them.
How many times can you score 60?

ANSWER 22

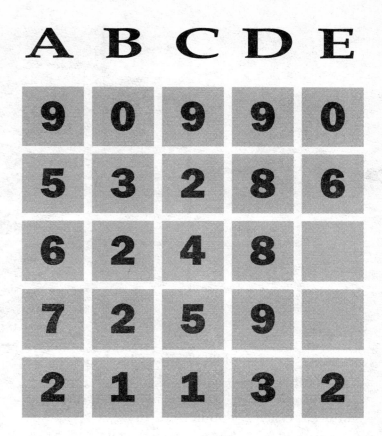

A	B	C	D	E
9	0	9	9	0
5	3	2	8	6
6	2	4	8	
7	2	5	9	
2	1	1	3	2

NUMBER PUZZLE 89

There is a relationship between the columns of
numbers in this diagram. The letters above the grid
are there to help you.
Which number should be placed in the
empty squares?

ANSWER 64

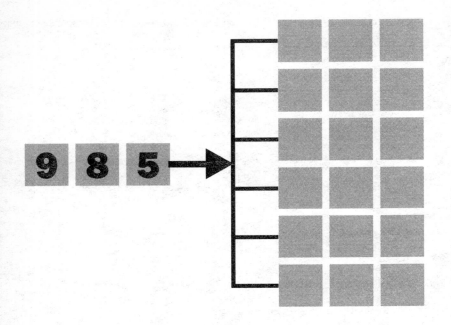

NUMBER PUZZLE 90

Place six three digit numbers of 100 plus at the end of 985 so that six numbers of six digits are produced. When each number is divided by 133 six whole numbers can be found. Which numbers should be placed in the grid?

ANSWER 12

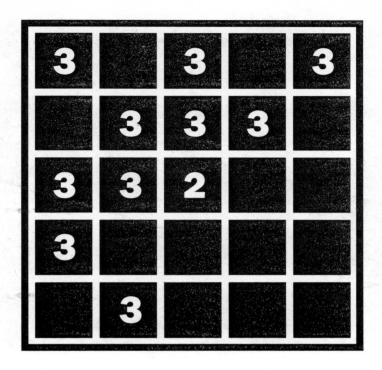

NUMBER PUZZLE 91

Each row, column and five-figure diagonal line
in this diagram must total 10. Three different
numbers must be used, as many times as necessary,
to achieve this.
What are the numbers?

ANSWER 53

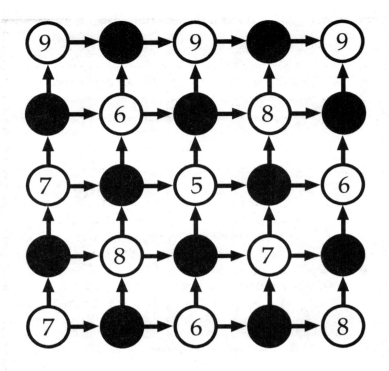

NUMBER PUZZLE 92

Move from the bottom left-hand corner to the top
right-hand corner following the arrows. Add the
numbers on your route together. If each black spot
is worth minus 4, what is the lowest number
you can score?

ANSWER 1

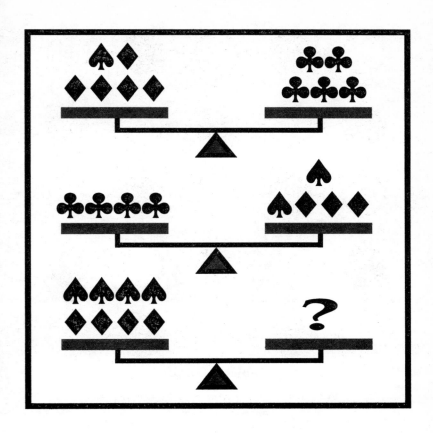

NUMBER PUZZLE 93

The top two scales are in perfect balance.
How many clubs will be needed to balance the
bottom set?

ANSWER 42

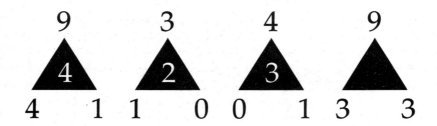

NUMBER PUZZLE 94

Which figure should be placed in the
empty triangle?

ANSWER 94

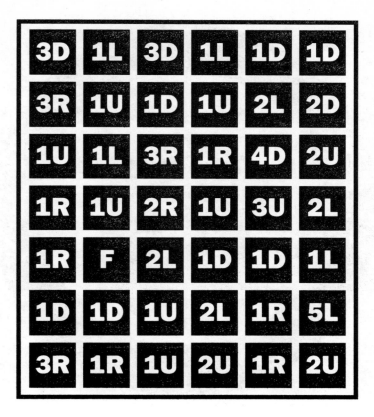

3D	1L	3D	1L	1D	1D
3R	1U	1D	1U	2L	2D
1U	1L	3R	1R	4D	2U
1R	1U	2R	1U	3U	2L
1R	F	2L	1D	1D	1L
1D	1D	1U	2L	1R	5L
3R	1R	1U	2U	1R	2U

NUMBER PUZZLE 95

Here is an unusual safe. Each of the buttons must
be pressed once only in the correct order to open it.
The last button is always marked F. The number of
moves and the direction is marked on each button.
Thus 1U would mean one move upwards
whilst 1L would mean one move to the left.
Which button is the first you must press?

ANSWER 83

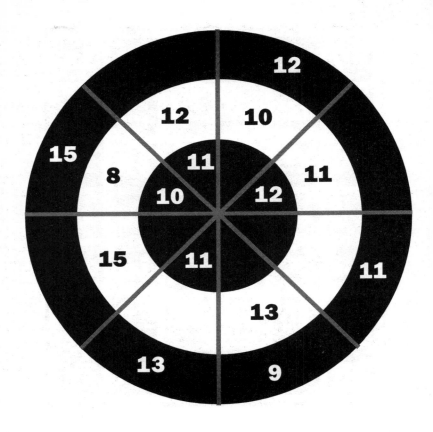

NUMBER PUZZLE 96

Complete the grid in such a way that each segment
of three numbers totals the same.
When this has been done correctly each of the three
concentric circles of eight numbers will produce
three identical totals.
Now complete the diagram.

ANSWER 31

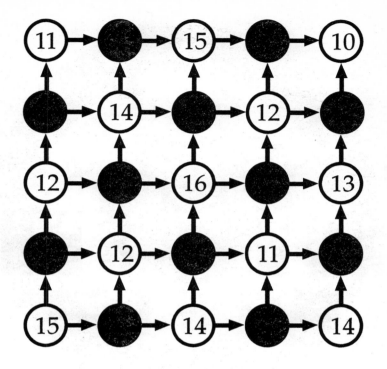

NUMBER PUZZLE 97

Move from the bottom left-hand corner to the top right-hand corner following the arrows. Add the numbers on your route together. If each black spot is worth minus 3, which number can be scored only once?

ANSWER 73

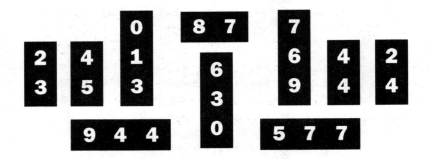

NUMBER PUZZLE 98

Place the tiles in a square to give some five-figure
numbers. When this has been done accurately the
same five numbers can be read both down and
across. How does the finished square look?

ANSWER 21

NUMBER PUZZLE 99

Start in the middle circle and move from circle to touching circle. Collect the four numbers which will total 30. Once a route has been found return to the middle circle and start again.
If a route can be found, which obeys the above rules but follows both a clockwise and an anticlockwise path, it is treated as two different routes. How many different ways are there?

ANSWER 63

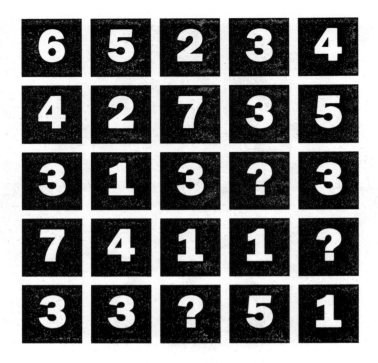

NUMBER PUZZLE 100

Which number should replace the question marks
in the diagram?

ANSWER 11

NUMBER PUZZLE 101

You have four shots with each go to score 62. Aim at this target and work out how many different ways there are to make the score. Assume each shot scores and once four numbers have been used the same four cannot be used again in another order. How many are there?

ANSWER 52

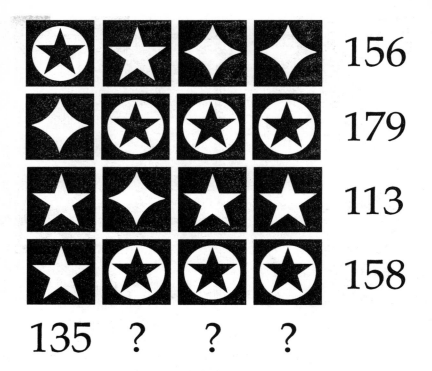

156

179

113

158

135   ?   ?   ?

NUMBER PUZZLE 102

The contents of each box has a value. The total of
the values is shown alongside a row or beneath a
column. Which number should replace the
question mark?

ANSWER 104

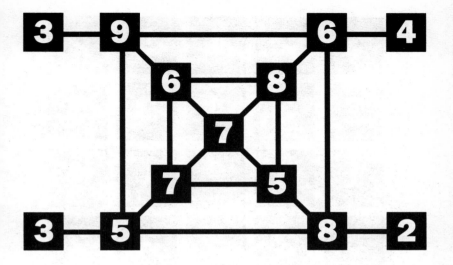

NUMBER PUZZLE 103

Start at the corner number and collect another four
numbers by following the paths shown. Add the
five numbers together. What is the lowest number
you can score and how many times can you
score it?

ANSWER 93

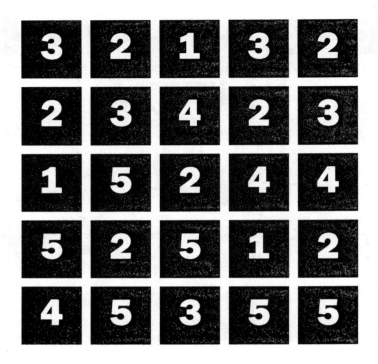

NUMBER PUZZLE 104

Move from square to adjacent square either
vertically or horizontally. Begin at the bottom
left-hand square and end at the top right-hand
square. Collect nine numbers and total them.
How many different ways are there to total 31?

ANSWER 41

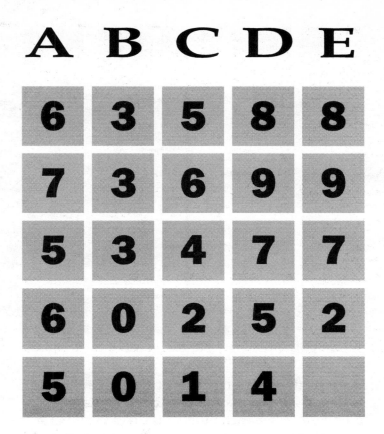

A	B	C	D	E
6	3	5	8	8
7	3	6	9	9
5	3	4	7	7
6	0	2	5	2
5	0	1	4	

NUMBER PUZZLE 105

There is a relationship between the columns of
numbers in this diagram. The letters above the grid
are there to help you. Which number should be
placed in the empty squares?

ANSWER 167

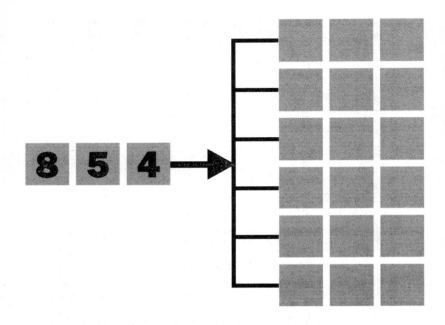

NUMBER PUZZLE 106

Place six three digit numbers of 100 plus at the end
of 854 so that six numbers of six digits are
produced. When each number is divided by 149 six
whole numbers can be found. Which numbers
should be placed in the grid?

ANSWER 115

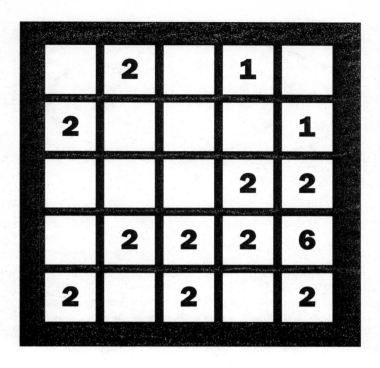

NUMBER PUZZLE 107

Each row, column and five-figure diagonal line
in this diagram must total 15. Three different
numbers must be used, as many times as necessary,
to achieve this.
What are the numbers?

ANSWER 187

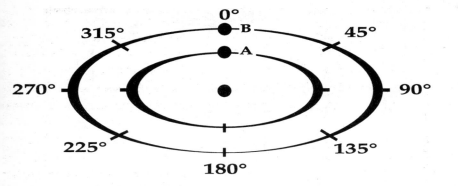

NUMBER PUZZLE 108

Two planets are in line with each other and the sun. The outer planet will orbit the sun every one hundred years. The inner planet takes twenty years. Both move in a clockwise direction. When will they next form a straight line with each other and the sun? The diagram should help you.

ANSWER 156

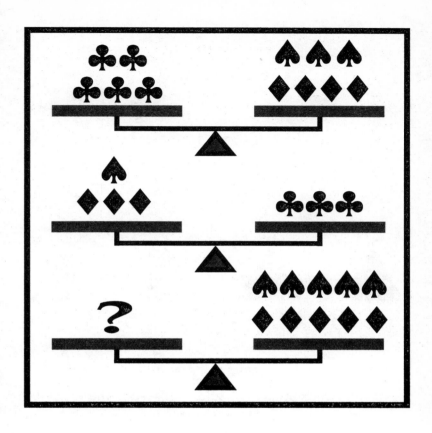

NUMBER PUZZLE 109

The top two scales are in perfect balance.
How many clubs will be needed to balance the
bottom set?

ANSWER 197

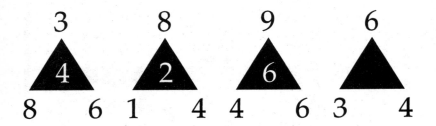

NUMBER PUZZLE 110

Which number should be placed in the empty triangle?

ANSWER 145

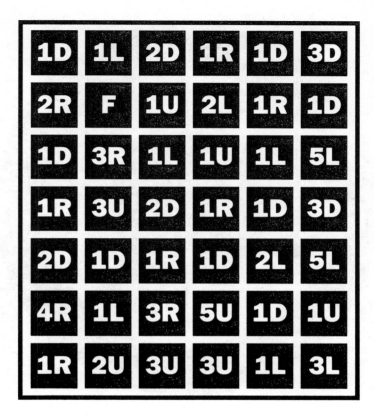

1D	1L	2D	1R	1D	3D
2R	F	1U	2L	1R	1D
1D	3R	1L	1U	1L	5L
1R	3U	2D	1R	1D	3D
2D	1D	1R	1D	2L	5L
4R	1L	3R	5U	1D	1U
1R	2U	3U	3U	1L	3L

NUMBER PUZZLE 111

Here is an unusual safe. Each of the buttons must
be pressed once only in the correct order to open it.
The last button is always marked F. The number of
moves and the direction is marked on each button.
Thus 1U would mean one move up
whilst 1L would mean one move to the left.
Which button is the first you must press?

ANSWER 166

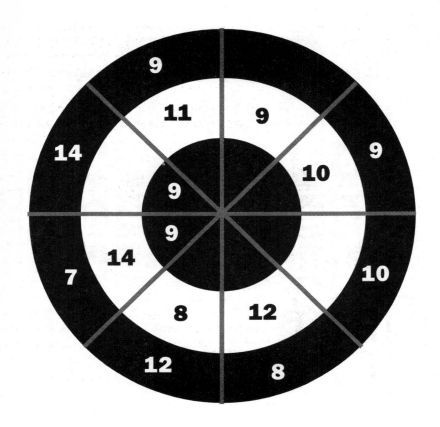

NUMBER PUZZLE 112

Complete the grid in such a way that each segment
of three numbers totals the same.
When this has been done correctly each of the three
concentric circles of eight numbers will produce
identical totals. Now complete the diagram.

ANSWER 114

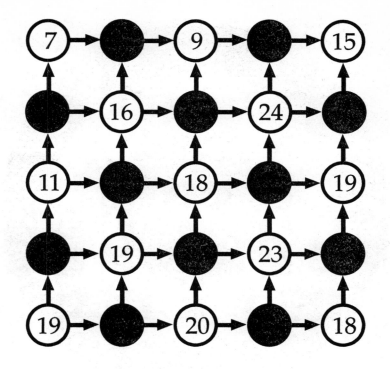

NUMBER PUZZLE 113

Move from the bottom left-hand corner to the top right-hand corner following the arrows. Add the numbers on your route together. If each black spot is worth minus 17, how many different routes are there to score 2?

ANSWER 135

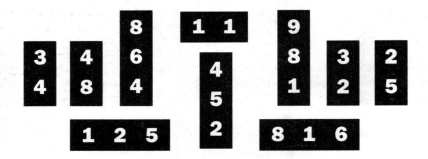

NUMBER PUZZLE 114

Place the tiles in a square to give some five-figure numbers. When this has been done accurately the same five numbers can be read both down and across. How does the finished square look?

ANSWER 155

NUMBER PUZZLE 115

Start in the middle circle and move from circle to touching circle. Collect the four numbers which will total 10. Once a route has been found return to the middle circle and start again.
If a route can be found, which obeys the above rules but follows both a clockwise and an anticlockwise path, it is treated as two different routes. How many different ways are there?

ANSWER 196

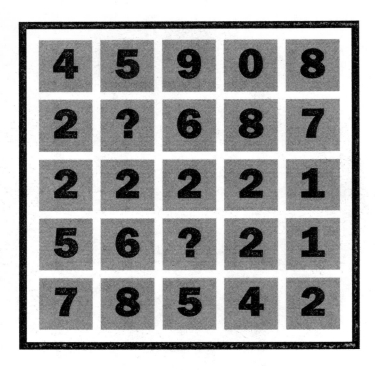

NUMBER PUZZLE 116

Which number should replace the question marks
in the diagram?

ANSWER 144

NUMBER PUZZLE 117

You have five shots with each go to score 22. Aim at this target and work out how many different ways there are to make the score. Assume each shot scores and once five numbers have been used the same five cannot be used again in another order. How many are there?

ANSWER 186

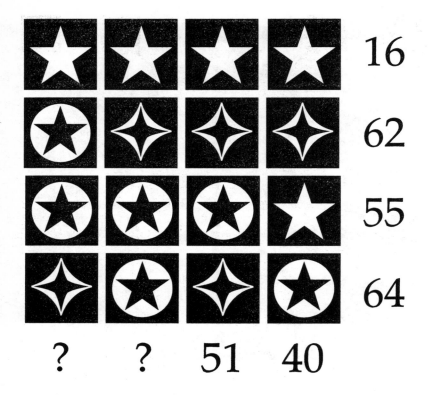

16

62

55

64

?   ?   51   40

NUMBER PUZZLE 118

The contents of each box has a value. The total of
the values is shown alongside a row or beneath a
column. Which number should replace the
question marks?

ANSWER 134

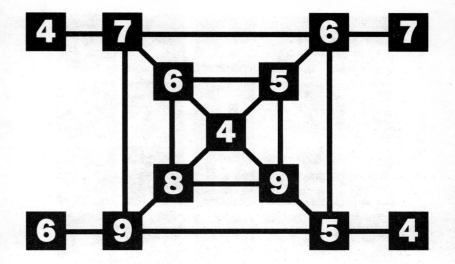

NUMBER PUZZLE 119

Start at any corner number and collect another four
numbers by following the paths shown. Add the
five numbers together.
How many times can you score 37?

ANSWER 176

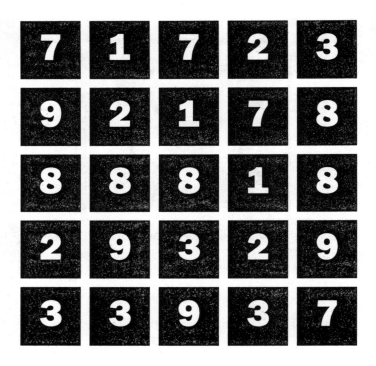

NUMBER PUZZLE 120

Move from square to adjacent square either
vertically or horizontally. Begin at the bottom
left-hand square and end at the top right-hand
square. Collect nine numbers and total them.
How many different ways are there to total 46?

ANSWER 124

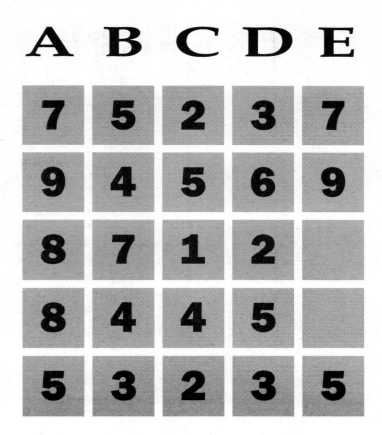

A B C D E

A	B	C	D	E
7	5	2	3	7
9	4	5	6	9
8	7	1	2	
8	4	4	5	
5	3	2	3	5

NUMBER PUZZLE 121

There is a relationship between the columns of
numbers in this diagram. The letters above the grid
are there to help you. Which number should be
placed in the empty squares?

ANSWER 165

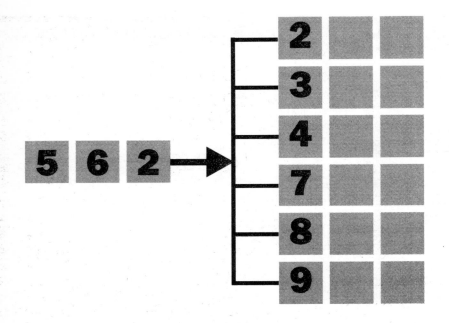

NUMBER PUZZLE 122

Place six three digit numbers of 100 plus at the end
of 562 so that six numbers of six digits are
produced. When each number is divided by
61.5 six whole numbers can be found. In this case,
the first numbers are given. Which numbers should
be placed in the grid?

ANSWER 113

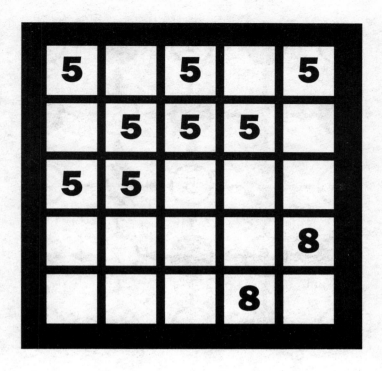

NUMBER PUZZLE 123

Each row, column and five-figure diagonal line
in this diagram must total 20. Three different
numbers must be used, as many times as necessary,
to achieve this.
What are the numbers?

ANSWER 125

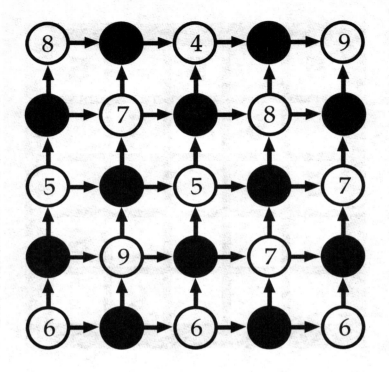

NUMBER PUZZLE 124

Move from the bottom left-hand corner to the top right-hand corner following the arrows. Add the numbers on your route together. If each black spot is worth minus 3, how many different ways can you score 20?

ANSWER 154

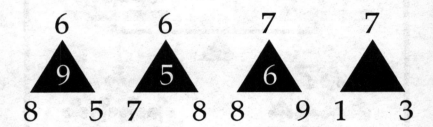

6   6   7   7

9   5   6

8   5   7   8   8   9   1   3

NUMBER PUZZLE 125

Which figure should be placed in the
empty triangle?

ANSWER 143

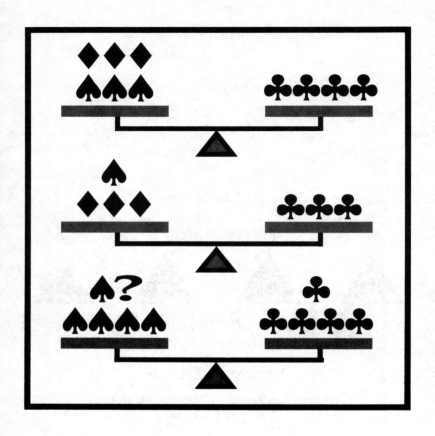

NUMBER PUZZLE 126

The top two scales are in perfect balance.
How many diamonds will be needed to balance the
bottom set?

ANSWER 195

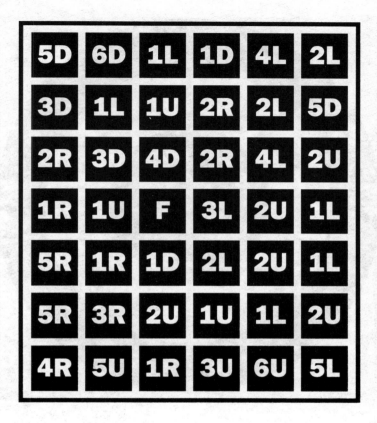

NUMBER PUZZLE 127

Here is an unusual safe. Each of the buttons must
be pressed once only in the correct order to open it.
The last button is always marked F. The number of
moves and the direction is marked on each button.
Thus 1U would mean one move up
whilst 1L would mean one move to the left.
Which button is the first you must press?

ANSWER 185

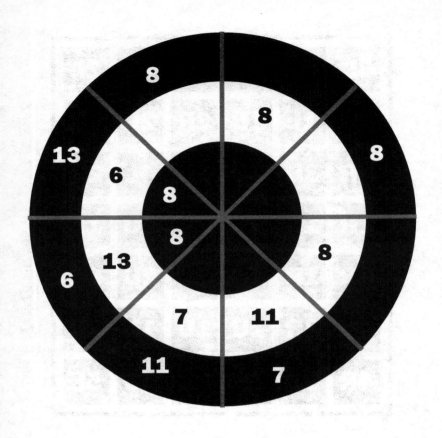

NUMBER PUZZLE 128

Complete the grid in such a way that each segment
of three numbers totals the same.
When this has been done correctly each of the three
concentric circles of eight numbers will produce
identical totals.
Now complete the diagram.

ANSWER 133

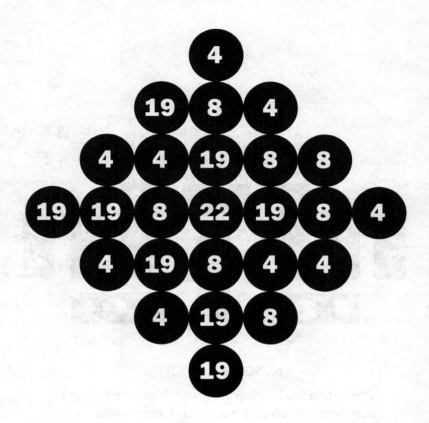

NUMBER PUZZLE 129

Start in the middle circle and move from circle to touching circle. Collect the four numbers which will total 53. Once a route has been found return to the middle circle and start again.

If a route can be found, which obeys the above rules but follows both a clockwise and an anticlockwise path, it is treated as two different routes. How many different ways are there?

ANSWER 175

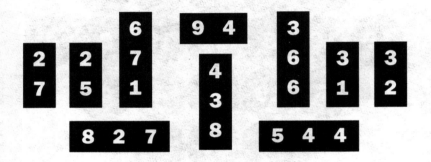

NUMBER PUZZLE 130

Place the tiles in a square to give some five-figure
numbers. When this has been done accurately the
same five numbers can be read both down and
across. How does the finished square look?

ANSWER 123

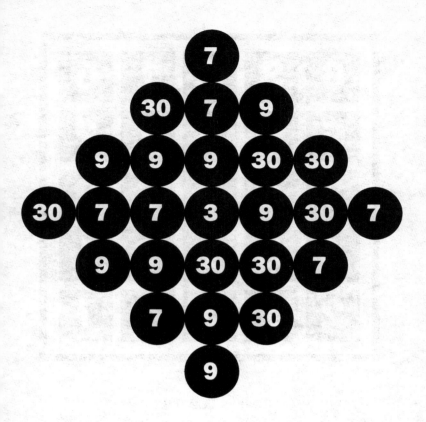

NUMBER PUZZLE 131

Start in the middle circle and move from circle to touching circle. Collect the four numbers which will total 49. Once a route has been found return to the middle circle and start again.
If a route can be found, which obeys the above rules but follows both a clockwise and an anticlockwise path, it is treated as two different routes. How many different ways are there?

ANSWER 164

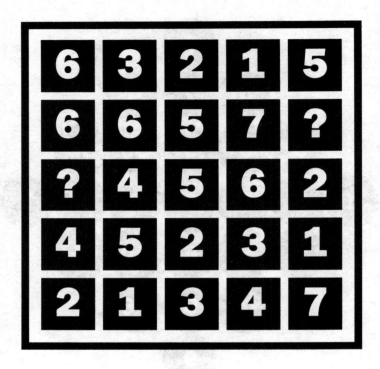

NUMBER PUZZLE 132

Which number should replace the question marks
in the diagram?

ANSWER 112

NUMBER PUZZLE 133

You have five shots with each go to score 61. Aim
at this target and work out how many different
ways there are to make the score. Assume each
shot scores and once five numbers have been used
the same five cannot be used again in another
order. How many ways are there?

ANSWER 177

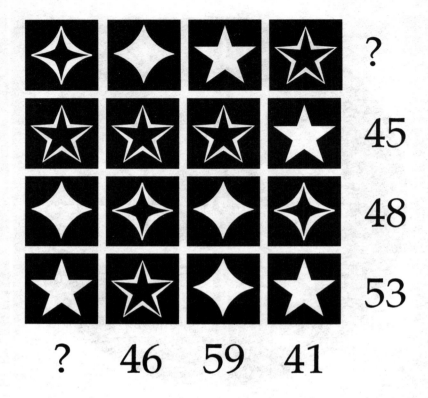

? 46 59 41

NUMBER PUZZLE 134

The contents of each box has a value. The total of
the values is shown alongside a row or beneath a
column. Which number should replace the
question marks?

ANSWER 153

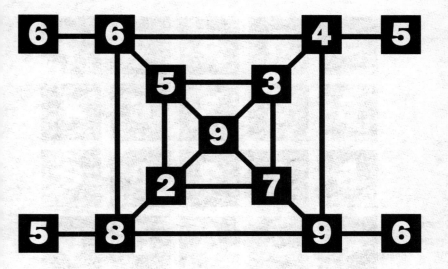

NUMBER PUZZLE 135

Start at any corner number and collect another four
numbers by following the paths shown. Add the
five numbers together.
How many times can you score 38?

ANSWER 194

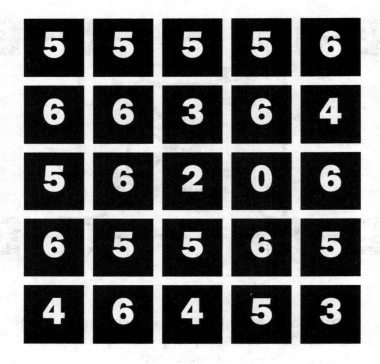

NUMBER PUZZLE 136

Move from square to adjacent square either vertically or horizontally. Begin at the bottom left-hand square and end at the top right-hand square. Collect nine numbers and total them. How many different ways are there to total 48?

ANSWER 142

A B C D E

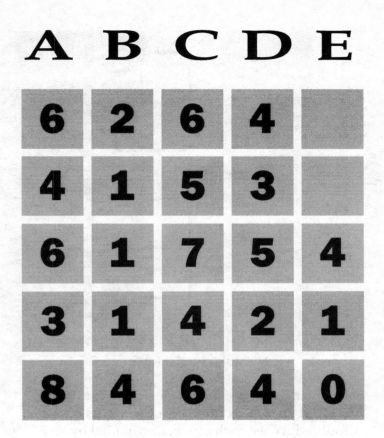

A	B	C	D	E
6	2	6	4	
4	1	5	3	
6	1	7	5	4
3	1	4	2	1
8	4	6	4	0

NUMBER PUZZLE 137

There is a relationship between the columns of numbers in this diagram. The letters above the grid are there to help you. Which number should be placed in the empty squares?

ANSWER 184

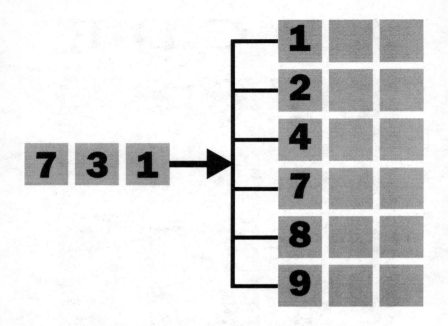

NUMBER PUZZLE 138

Place six three digit numbers of 100 plus at the end of 731 so that six numbers of six digits are produced. When each number is divided by 39.5 six whole numbers can be found. In this case, the first numbers are given.

Which numbers should be placed in the grid?

ANSWER 132

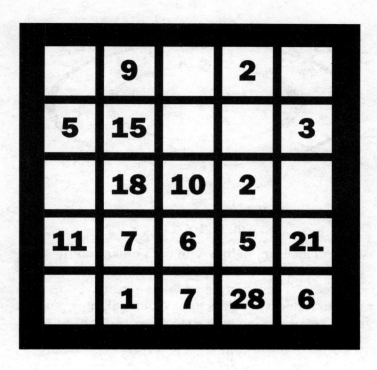

	9		2	
5	15			3
	18	10	2	
11	7	6	5	21
	1	7	28	6

NUMBER PUZZLE 139

Each row, column and five-figure diagonal line
in this diagram must total 50. Four different
numbers must be used, as many times as necessary,
to achieve this.
What are the numbers?

ANSWER 174

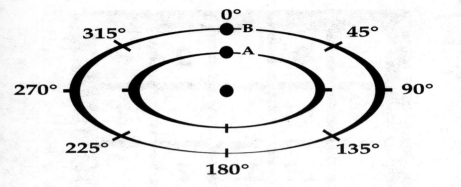

NUMBER PUZZLE 140

Two planets are in line with each other and the sun. The outer planet will orbit the sun every 36 years. The inner planet takes 4 years. Both move in a clockwise direction. When will they next form a straight line with each other and the sun? The diagram should help you.

ANSWER 122

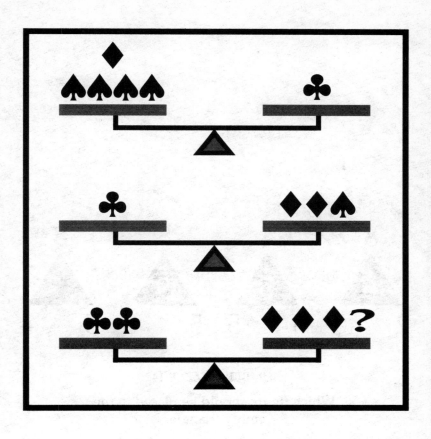

NUMBER PUZZLE 141

The top two scales are in perfect balance.
How many spades will be needed to balance the
bottom set?

ANSWER 163

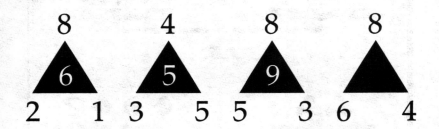

8   4   8   8

6   5   9

2   1   3   5   5   3   6   4

NUMBER PUZZLE 142

Which figure should be placed in the
empty triangle?

ANSWER 111

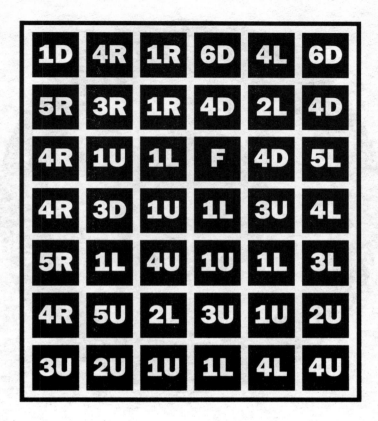

NUMBER PUZZLE 143

Here is an unusual safe. Each of the buttons must
be pressed once only in the correct order to open it.
The last button is always marked F. The number of
moves and the direction is marked on each button.
Thus 1U would mean one move up
whilst 1L would mean one move to the left.
Which button is the first you must press?

ANSWER 146

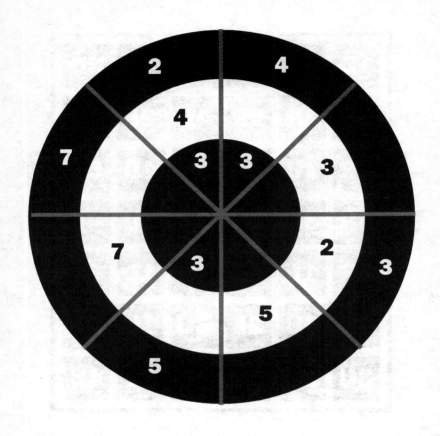

NUMBER PUZZLE 144

Complete the grid in such a way that each segment of three numbers totals the same.
When this has been done correctly each of the three concentric circles of eight numbers will produce identical totals.
Now complete the diagram.

ANSWER 152

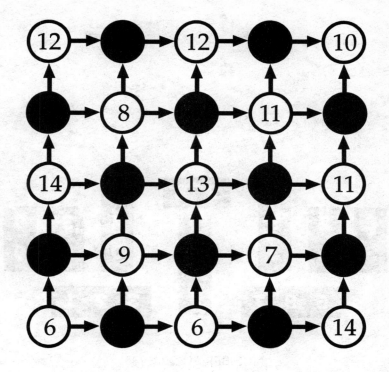

NUMBER PUZZLE 145

Move from the bottom left-hand corner to the top right-hand corner following the arrows. Add the numbers on your route together. If each black spot is worth minus 7, how many different times can you score 22?

ANSWER 193

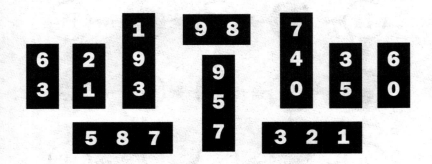

NUMBER PUZZLE 146

Place the tiles in a square to give some five-figure
numbers. When this has been done accurately the
same five numbers can be read both down and
across. How does the finished square look?

ANSWER 141

NUMBER PUZZLE 147

Start in the middle circle and move from circle to touching circle. Collect the four numbers which will total 45. Once a route has been found return to the middle circle and start again.

If a route can be found, which obeys the above rules but follows both a clockwise and an anticlockwise path, it is treated as two different routes. How many different ways are there?

ANSWER 183

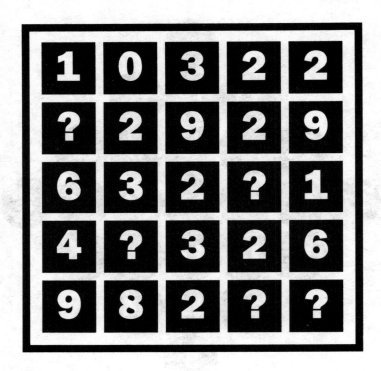

NUMBER PUZZLE 148

Which number should replace the question marks
in the diagram?

ANSWER 131

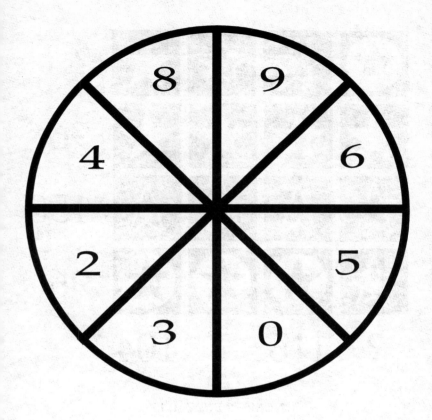

NUMBER PUZZLE 149

You have three shots with each go to score 18. Aim
at this target and work out how many different
ways there are to make the score. Assume each
shot scores and once three numbers have been used
the same three cannot be used again
in another order.
How many are there?

ANSWER 173

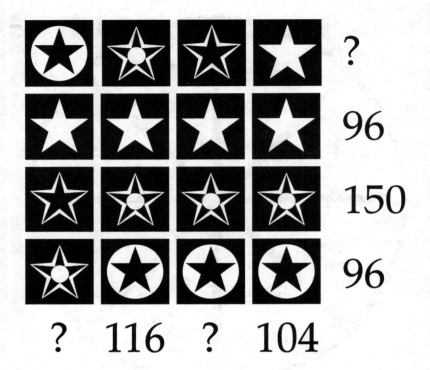

NUMBER PUZZLE 150

The contents of each box has a value. The total of the values is shown alongside a row or beneath a column. Which number should replace the question marks?

ANSWER 121

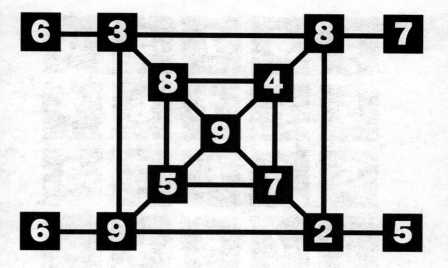

NUMBER PUZZLE 151

Start at any corner number and collect another four
numbers by following the paths shown. Add the
five numbers together.
How many ways can you score 36?

ANSWER 162

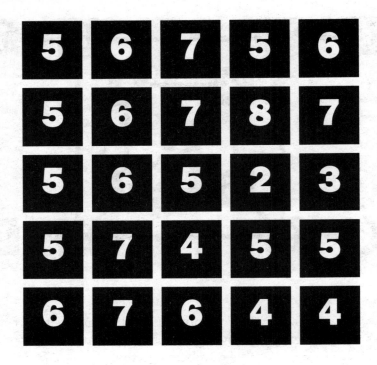

NUMBER PUZZLE 152

Move from square to adjacent square either
vertically or horizontally. Begin at the bottom
left-hand square and end at the top right-hand
square. Collect nine numbers and total them.
What is the highest score possible?

ANSWER 110

A B C D E

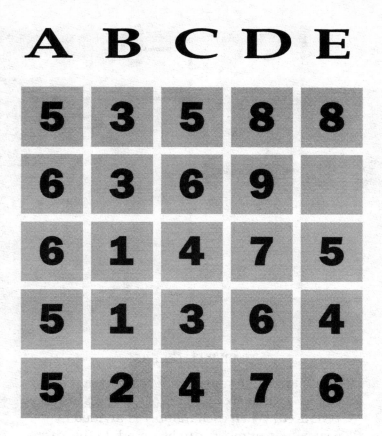

A	B	C	D	E
5	3	5	8	8
6	3	6	9	
6	1	4	7	5
5	1	3	6	4
5	2	4	7	6

NUMBER PUZZLE 153

There is a relationship between the columns of numbers in this diagram. The letters above the grid are there to help you. Which number should be placed in the empty square?

ANSWER 198

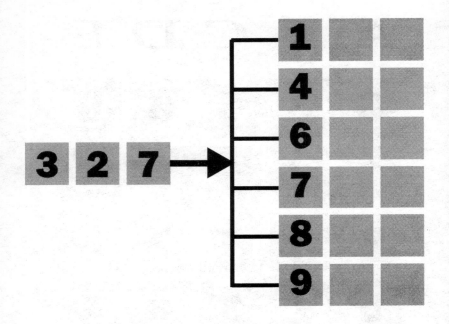

NUMBER PUZZLE 154

Place six three digit numbers of 100 plus at the end
of 327 so that six numbers of six digits are
produced. When each number is divided by
27.5 six whole numbers can be found. In this case,
the first numbers are given. Which numbers should
be placed inthe grid?

ANSWER 151

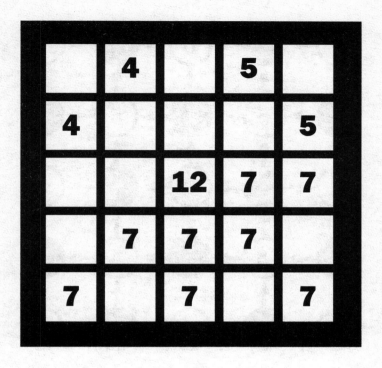

NUMBER PUZZLE 155

Each row, column and five-figure diagonal line
in this diagram must total 60. Three different
numbers must be used, as many times as necessary,
to achieve this. What are the numbers?

ANSWER 192

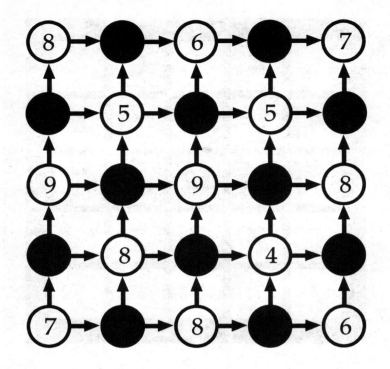

NUMBER PUZZLE 156

Move from the bottom left-hand corner to the top right-hand corner following the arrows. Add the numbers on your route together. If each black spot is worth 13, which two numbers can be scored once only?

ANSWER 140

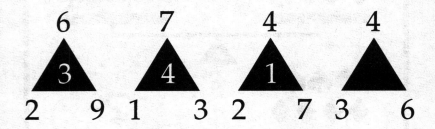

NUMBER PUZZLE 157

Which figure should be placed in the
empty triangle?

ANSWER 130

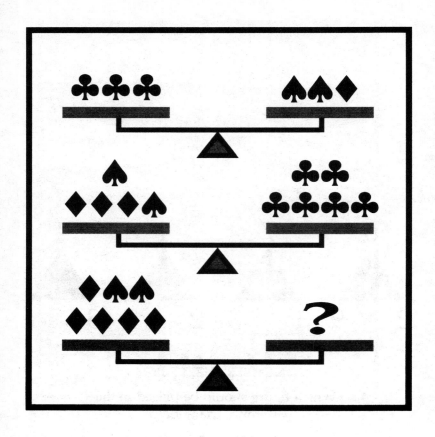

NUMBER PUZZLE 158

The top two scales are in perfect balance.
How many clubs will be needed to balance the
bottom set?

ANSWER 182

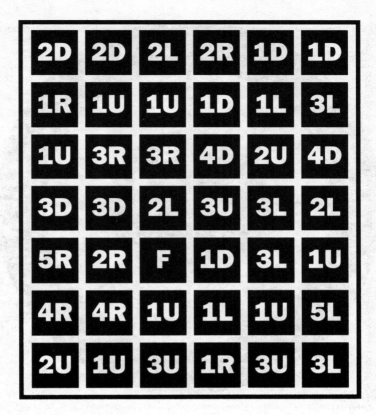

2D	2D	2L	2R	1D	1D
1R	1U	1U	1D	1L	3L
1U	3R	3R	4D	2U	4D
3D	3D	2L	3U	3L	2L
5R	2R	F	1D	3L	1U
4R	4R	1U	1L	1U	5L
2U	1U	3U	1R	3U	3L

NUMBER PUZZLE 159

Here is an unusual safe. Each of the buttons must
be pressed once only in the correct order to open it.
The last button is always marked F. The number of
moves and the direction is marked on each button.
Thus 1U would mean one move up
whilst 1L would mean one move to the left.
Which button is the first you must press?

ANSWER 172

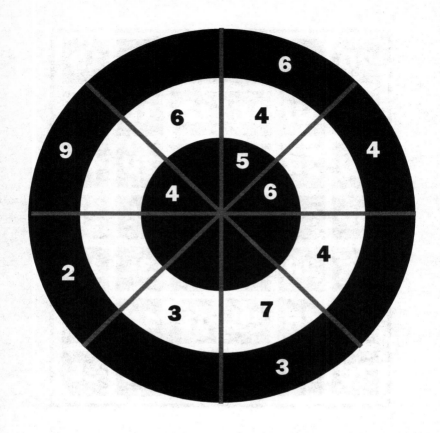

NUMBER PUZZLE 160

Complete the grid in such a way that each segment of three numbers totals the same.
When this has been done correctly each of the three concentric circles of eight numbers will produce identical totals.
Now complete the diagram.

ANSWER 120

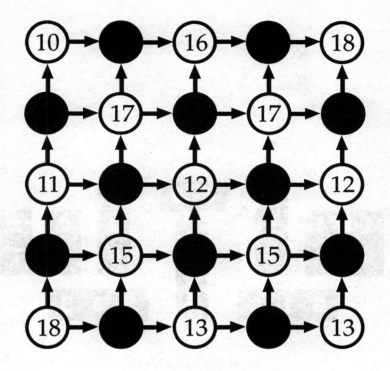

NUMBER PUZZLE 161

Move from the bottom left-hand corner to the top
right-hand corner following the arrows. Add the
numbers on your route together. If each black spot is
worth minus 9, how many times can you score 41?

ANSWER 161

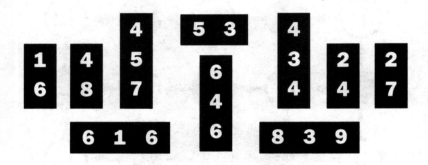

NUMBER PUZZLE 162

Place the tiles in a square to give some five-figure
numbers. When this has been done accurately the
same five numbers can be read both down and
across. How does the finished square look?

ANSWER 109

NUMBER PUZZLE 163

Start in the middle circle and move from circle to
touching circle. Collect the four numbers which
will total 75. Once a route has been found return to
the middle circle and start again.
If a route can be found, which obeys the above
rules but follows both a clockwise and an
anticlockwise path, it is treated as two different
routes. How many different ways are there?

ANSWER 202

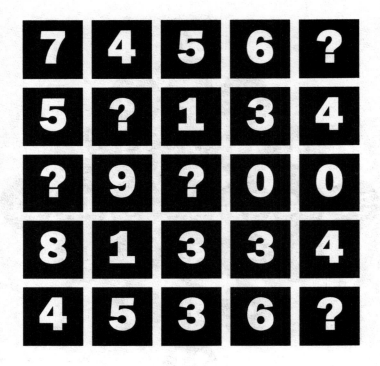

NUMBER PUZZLE 164

Which number should replace the question marks
in the diagram?

ANSWER 150

NUMBER PUZZLE 165

You have five shots with each go to score 56. Aim
at this target and work out how many different
ways there are to make the score. Assume each
shot scores and once five numbers have been used
the same five cannot be used again in another
order. How many ways are there?

ANSWER 191

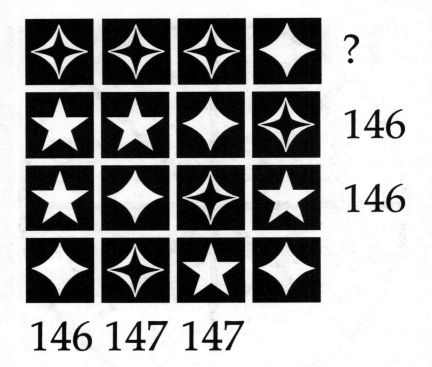

146 147 147

NUMBER PUZZLE 166

The contents of each box has a value. The total of
the values is shown alongside a row or beneath a
column. Which number should replace the
question mark?

ANSWER 139

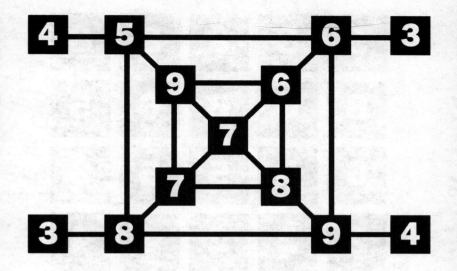

NUMBER PUZZLE 167

Start at any corner number and collect another four numbers by following the paths shown. Add the five numbers together. How many times can you score less than 30?

ANSWER 181

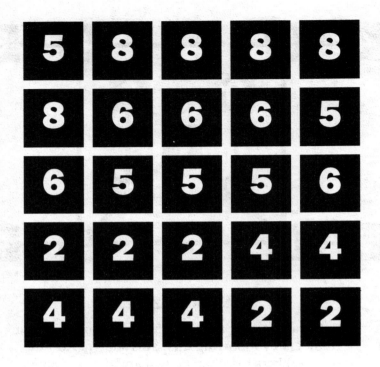

NUMBER PUZZLE 168

Move from square to adjacent square either vertically or horizontally. Begin at the bottom left-hand square and end at the top right-hand square. Collect nine numbers and total them. What are the highest and lowest numbers you can score?

ANSWER 129

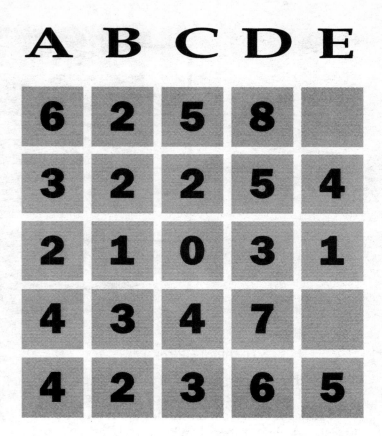

A B C D E

A	B	C	D	E
6	2	5	8	
3	2	2	5	4
2	1	0	3	1
4	3	4	7	
4	2	3	6	5

NUMBER PUZZLE 169

There is a relationship between the columns of numbers in this diagram. The letters above the grid are there to help you. Which number should be placed in the empty squares?

ANSWER 171

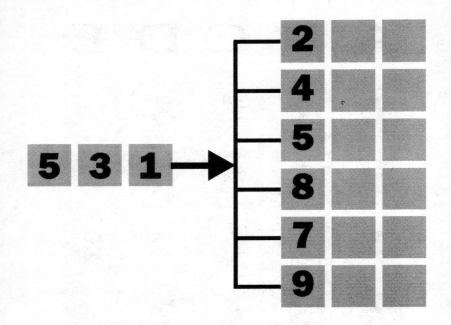

NUMBER PUZZLE 170

Place six three digit numbers of 100 plus at the end
of 531 so that six numbers of six digits are
produced. When each number is divided by
40.5 six whole numbers can be found. In this case,
the first numbers are given. Which numbers should
be placed inthe grid?

ANSWER 119

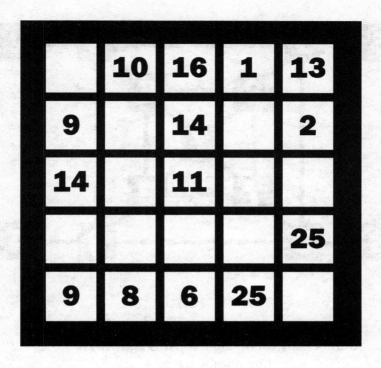

NUMBER PUZZLE 171

Each row, column and five-figure diagonal line
in this diagram must total 55. Three different
numbers must be used, as many times as necessary,
to achieve this.
What are these numbers?

ANSWER 160

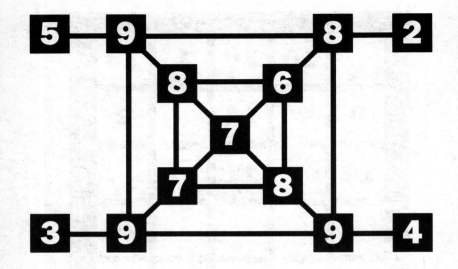

NUMBER PUZZLE 172

Start at any corner number and collect another four
numbers by following the paths shown. Add the
five numbers together.
How many times can you score 40?

ANSWER 108

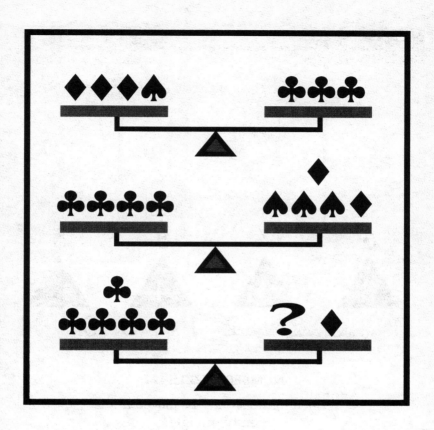

NUMBER PUZZLE 173

The top two scales are in perfect balance.
How many spades will be needed to balance the
bottom set?

ANSWER 201

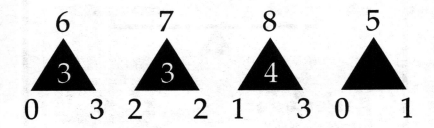

6   7   8   5

3   3   4

0   3   2   2   1   3   0   1

NUMBER PUZZLE 174

Which figure should be placed in the empty triangle?

ANSWER 149

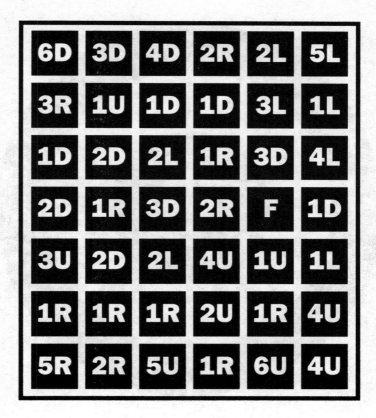

6D	3D	4D	2R	2L	5L
3R	1U	1D	1D	3L	1L
1D	2D	2L	1R	3D	4L
2D	1R	3D	2R	F	1D
3U	2D	2L	4U	1U	1L
1R	1R	1R	2U	1R	4U
5R	2R	5U	1R	6U	4U

NUMBER PUZZLE 175

Here is an unusual safe. Each of the buttons must
be pressed once only in the correct order to open it.
The last button is always marked F. The number of
moves and the direction is marked on each button.
Thus 1U would mean one move up
whilst 1L would mean one move to the left.
Which button is the first you must press?

ANSWER 190

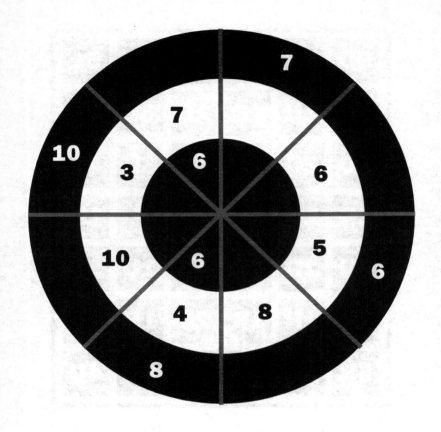

NUMBER PUZZLE 176

Complete the grid in such a way that each segment
of three numbers totals the same.
When this has been done correctly each of the three
concentric circles of eight numbers will produce
identical totals.
Now complete the diagram.

ANSWER 138

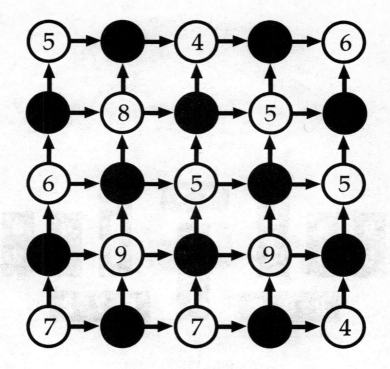

NUMBER PUZZLE 177

Move from the bottom left-hand corner to the top
right-hand corner following the arrows. Add the
numbers on your route together. If each black spot
is worth 11, how many times can you score 80?

ANSWER 180

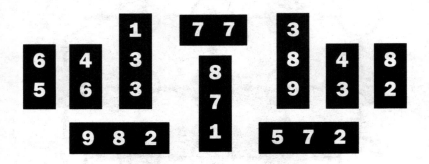

NUMBER PUZZLE 178

Place the tiles in the square to give some five-figure
numbers. When this has been done accurately the
same five numbers can be read both down and
across. How does the finished square look?

ANSWER 128

NUMBER PUZZLE 179

Start in the middle circle and move from circle to touching circle. Collect the four numbers which will total 83. Once a route has been found return to the middle circle and start again.

If a route can be found, which obeys the above rules but follows both a clockwise and an anticlockwise path, it is treated as two different routes. How many different ways are there?

ANSWER 170

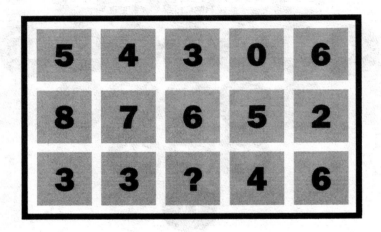

NUMBER PUZZLE 180

Which number should replace the question mark in
the diagram?

ANSWER 118

NUMBER PUZZLE 181

You have five shots with each go to score 44. Aim at this target and work out how many different ways there are to make the score. Assume each shot scores and once five numbers have been used the same five cannot be used again in another order. How many ways are there?

ANSWER 159

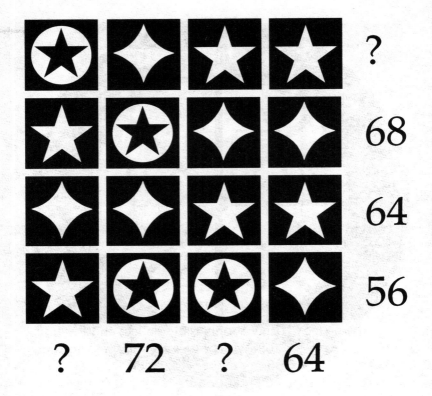

? 68 64 56

? 72 ? 64

NUMBER PUZZLE 182

The contents of each box has a value. The total of the values is shown alongside a row or beneath a column. Which number should replace the question marks?

ANSWER 107

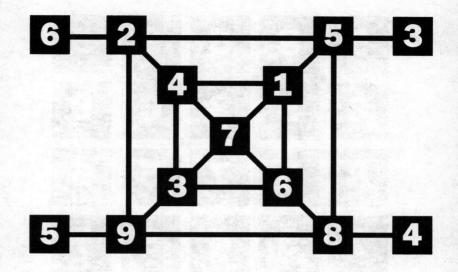

NUMBER PUZZLE 183

Start at any corner number and collect another four
numbers by following the paths shown. Add the
five numbers together.
What is the lowest number you can score?

ANSWER 200

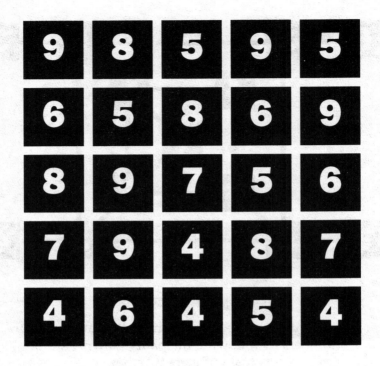

NUMBER PUZZLE 184

Move from square to adjacent square either
vertically or horizontally. Begin at the bottom
left-hand square and end at the top right-hand
square. Collect nine numbers and total them.
Which total can be scored only once?

ANSWER 148

A B C D E

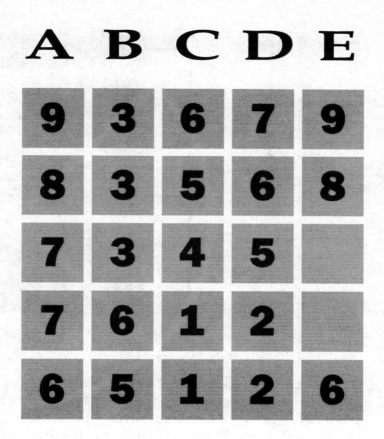

A	B	C	D	E
9	3	6	7	9
8	3	5	6	8
7	3	4	5	
7	6	1	2	
6	5	1	2	6

NUMBER PUZZLE 185

There is a relationship between the columns of numbers in this diagram. The letters above the grid are there to help you. Which number should be placed in the empty squares?

ANSWER 189

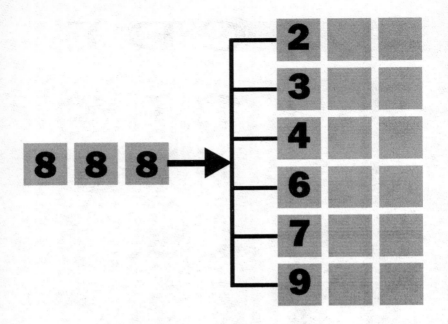

NUMBER PUZZLE 186

Place six three digit numbers of 100 plus at the end of 888 so that six numbers of six digits are produced. When each number is divided by 77 six whole numbers can be found. In this case, the first numbers are given. Which numbers should be placed inthe grid?

ANSWER 137

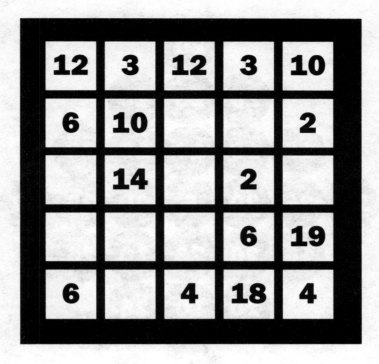

NUMBER PUZZLE 187

Each row, column and five-figure diagonal line in this diagram must total 40. Three different numbers must be used, as many times as necessary, to achieve this.
What are the numbers?

ANSWER 179

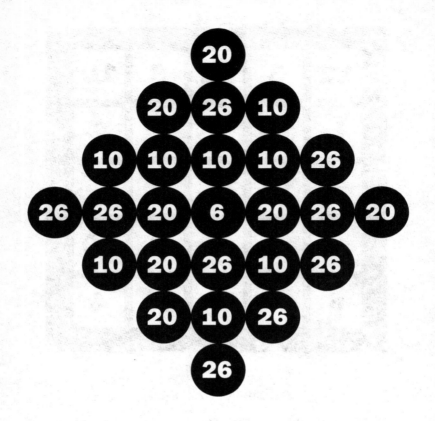

NUMBER PUZZLE 188

Start in the middle circle and move from circle to touching circle. Collect the four numbers which will total 62. Once a route has been found return to the middle circle and start again.

If a route can be found, which obeys the above rules but follows both a clockwise and an anticlockwise path, it is treated as two different routes. How many different ways are there?

ANSWER 127

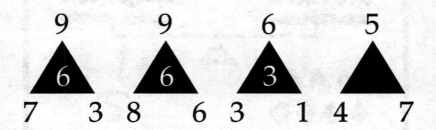

9   9   6   5

6   6   3

7   3   8   6   3   1   4   7

NUMBER PUZZLE 189

Which figure should be placed in the
empty triangle?

ANSWER 117

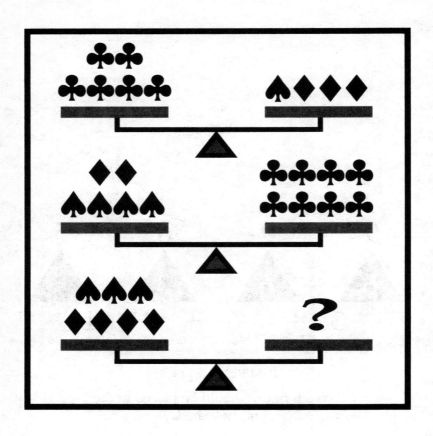

NUMBER PUZZLE 190

The top two scales are in perfect balance.
How many clubs will be needed to balance the
bottom set?

ANSWER 169

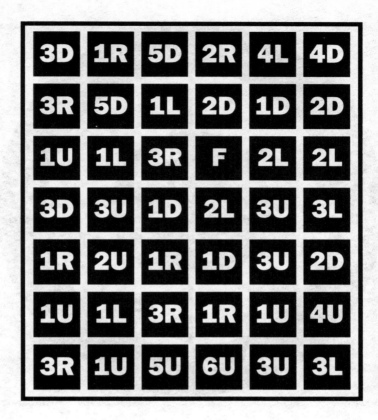

3D	1R	5D	2R	4L	4D
3R	5D	1L	2D	1D	2D
1U	1L	3R	F	2L	2L
3D	3U	1D	2L	3U	3L
1R	2U	1R	1D	3U	2D
1U	1L	3R	1R	1U	4U
3R	1U	5U	6U	3U	3L

NUMBER PUZZLE 191

Here is an unusual safe. Each of the buttons must
be pressed once only in the correct order to open it.
The last button is always marked F. The number of
moves and the direction is marked on each button.
Thus 1U would mean one move up
whilst 1L would mean one move to the left.
Which button is the first you must press?

ANSWER 158

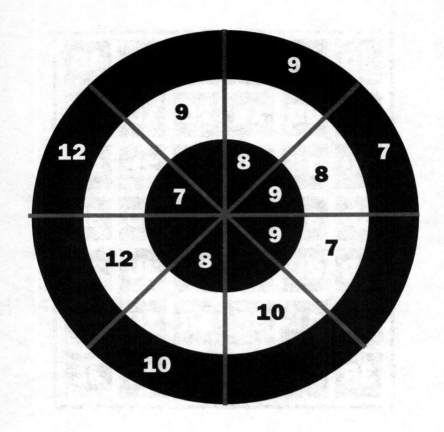

NUMBER PUZZLE 192

Complete the grid in such a way that each segment
of three numbers totals the same.
When this has been done correctly each of the three
concentric circles of eight numbers will produce
identical totals. Now complete the diagram.

ANSWER 106

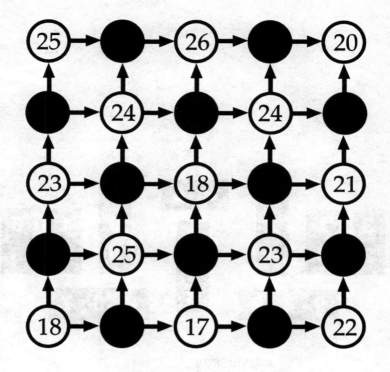

NUMBER PUZZLE 193

Move from the bottom left-hand corner to the top right-hand corner following the arrows. Add the numbers on your route together. If each black spot is worth minus 19, how many times can you score 24?

ANSWER 199

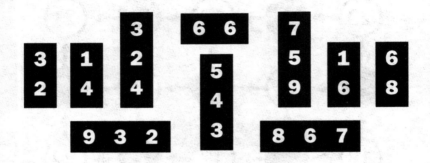

NUMBER PUZZLE 194

Place the tiles a square to give some five-figure
numbers. When this has been done accurately
the same five numbers can be read both down
and across. How does the finished square look?

ANSWER 147

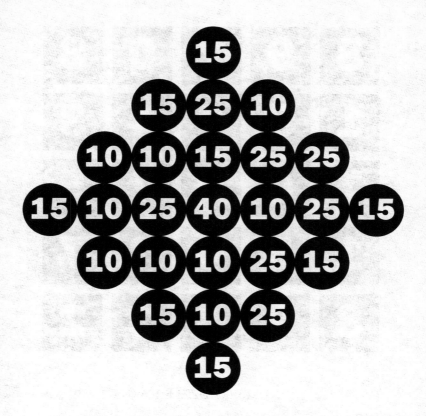

NUMBER PUZZLE 195

Start in the middle circle and move from circle to touching circle. Collect the four numbers which will total 90. Once a route has been found return to the middle circle and start again.
If a route can be found, which obeys the above rules but follows both a clockwise and an anticlockwise path, it is treated as two different routes. How many different ways are there?

ANSWER 188

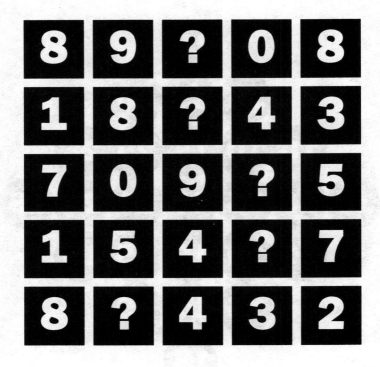

8	9	?	0	8
1	8	?	4	3
7	0	9	?	5
1	5	4	?	7
8	?	4	3	2

NUMBER PUZZLE 196

Which number should replace the question marks
in the diagram?

ANSWER 136

NUMBER PUZZLE 197

You have three shots with each go to score 36. Aim at this target and work out how many different ways there are to make the score. Assume each shot scores and once three numbers have been used the same three cannot be used again in another order. How many are there?

ANSWER 178

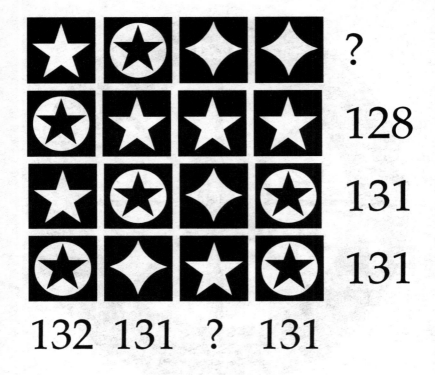

?

128

131

131

132 131 ? 131

The contents of each box has a value. The total of the values is shown alongside a row or beneath a column. Which numbers should replace the question marks?

ANSWER 126

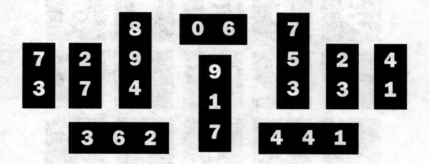

NUMBER PUZZLE 199

Place the tiles in a square to give some five-figure numbers. When this has been done accurately the same five numbers can be read both down and across. How does the finished square look?

ANSWER 168

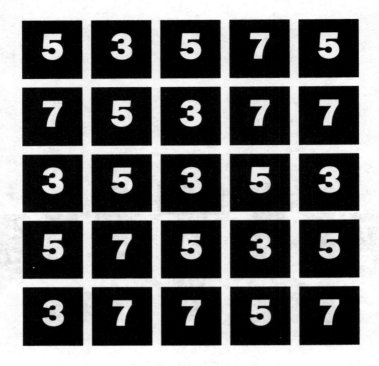

NUMBER PUZZLE 200

Move from square to adjacent square either
vertically or horizontally. Begin at the bottom
left-hand square and end at the top right-hand
square. Collect nine numbers and total them.
How many different ways are there to total 39?

ANSWER 116

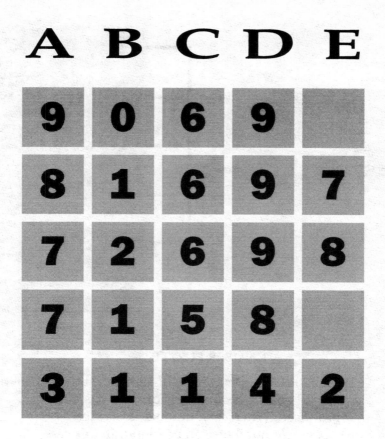

A B C D E

A	B	C	D	E
9	0	6	9	
8	1	6	9	7
7	2	6	9	8
7	1	5	8	
3	1	1	4	2

NUMBER PUZZLE 201

There is a relationship between the columns of numbers in this diagram. The letters above the grid are there to help you. Which number should be placed in the empty squares?

ANSWER 157

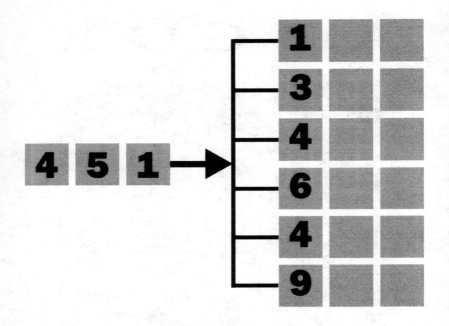

NUMBER PUZZLE 202

Place six three digit numbers of 100 plus at the end
of 451 so that six numbers of six digits are
produced. When each number is divided by
61 six whole numbers can be found. In this case,
the first numbers are given. Which numbers should
be placed in the grid?

ANSWER 105

Answers

1   17.

2

3   29.

4   10. The top number is multiplied by the bottom left-hand number and the total is divided by the bottom right-hand number.

5   1. The top row minus the bottom row gives the third row. The bottom row plus the second row gives the fourth row.

6   164
     295
     426
     557
     688
     819

7   Our answer is:

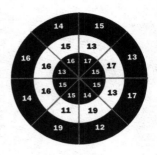

8   11 ways.

9   In two years time. The outer planet is 60 degrees in its orbit, the sun is in the middle and the inner planet is at 240 degrees.

10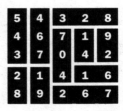

11   8. The top row minus the bottom row gives the third row.
The third row plus the second row gives the fourth row.

12   131
      264
      397
      663
      796
      929

13   Our answer is:

14   107 (values of symbols:
◇ = 18, ◆ = 30, ☆ = 29).

15   Once.

16

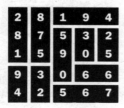

17   Once.

18   7. The top number is
multiplied by the bottom left
number and the bottom right
number is taken away from
this total to give the
middle number.

19   5. 3rd row - top row =
5th row. 4th row + 5th row =
2nd row.

20   162
      313
      464
      615
      766
      917

21

7	6	9	4	4
6	3	0	2	4
9	0	1	3	5
4	2	3	8	7
4	4	5	7	7

22   Three times.

23   4. The top number is added to the bottom left-hand number and the bottom right-hand number is subtracted.

24   6. The top row plus the second row gives the third row. The second row plus the fourth row gives the fifth row.

25   314
         425
         536
         647
         758
         869

26   Our answer is:

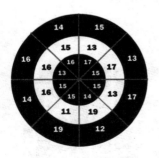

27   149 (values of symbols: ◈ = 35, ◆ = 42, ☆ = 37).

28   3 times.

29

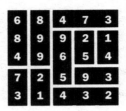

30   3 ways.

31   Our answer is:

32   65 (values of symbols: ✪ = 7, ◆ = 8, ★ = 25, ☆ = 17).

33   In three and three-quarter years' time. The outer planet is 90 degrees in its orbit, the sun is in the middle and the inner planet is at 270 degrees.

34

35   Once.

36   3. The top number minus the bottom left-hand number is multiplied by the bottom right-hand number.

37   1. The second row plus the third row gives the top row. The third row plus the fourth row gives the bottom row.

38   431
      542
      653
      764
      875
      986

39   Our answer is:

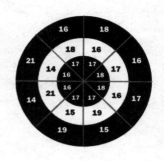

40   62 (values of symbols: = 13, ★ = 21, ◆ = 7).

41   6 ways.

42   7 clubs.

43   8. The middle row minus the bottom row equals the top row.

44   232
      354
      476
      598
      842
      964

45   Our answer is:

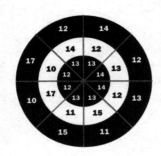

46   78 (values of symbols: ⊕ = 28, ★ = 13, ☆ = 9).

47   In one and a half years' time. The outer planet is 90 degrees in its orbit, the sun is in the middle and the inner planet is at 270 degrees.

48

49   2 ways.

50   6. The bottom two numbers are added and taken from the top number.

51   5. Take the bottom row from the middle row to give the top row.

52   27 ways.

53   0, 1 and 4.

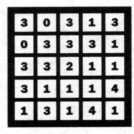

54   Four.

55   40.

56   4 spades.

57   10 ways.

58   2. A + B = D. A - B = C. D - C = E.

59   4U on the third row
from the bottom.

60   204 (values of symbols:
☆ = 44, ★ = 58, ◈ = 45).

61   10, 11, 23 and 31.

25	9	23	5	23
12	22	24	23	4
24	20	17	14	10
13	11	10	12	39
11	23	11	31	9

62   5 routes.

63   14 ways.

64   4. A + B = D.
A - B = C.
D - C = E.

65   1L in the second
column from the left one row
from thebottom.

66   8 ways.

67   9, 17 and 18.

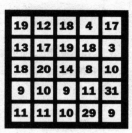

19	12	18	4	17
13	17	19	18	3
18	20	14	8	10
9	10	9	11	31
11	11	10	29	9

68   Four routes.

69   30.

70   7 clubs.

71   12 ways.

72   2. A + B = D.
A - B = C.
D - C = E.

73   58.

74   40 and once.

75   6 clubs.

76   7 ways.

77   4. A - B + 1 = D.

D - 1 = C.

D + B - 1 = E.

78   1L in the third column from the left on the third row from the bottom.

79   15 ways.

80   11, 12 and 21.

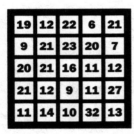

81   4 times.

82   37.

83   1U in the second column from the left on the second row.

84   7 ways.

85   9 and 17.

86   2 routes.

87   4 times.

88   4 diamonds.

89   7 ways.

90   3. A - B = D.

C = D + 2.

E = D - B.

91   1D fourth from the left on the top row.

92   11 ways.

93   27 and twice.

94   3. The top number minus the bottom left-hand number minus the bottom right-hand number.

95   7 ways.

96   5. A - B = D.
D + 2 = C.
D - B = E.

97   3U on the bottom row.

98   21 ways.

99   11, 18 and 19.

19	13	21	3	19
14	19	20	18	4
20	23	15	7	10
11	12	10	11	31
11	8	9	36	11

100   One.

101   Twice.

102   5 clubs.

103   5 ways.

104   157 (values of symbols: ★ = 45, ◆ = 44, ☆ = 23).

105.   156
339
461
644
400
949

106.   Our answer is:

107.   52 (values of symbols: ★ = 12, ☆ = 8, ◆ = 24).

108.   3 times.

109.

6	4	6	1	6
4	3	4	2	4
6	4	5	7	8
1	2	7	5	3
6	4	8	3	9

110.   60.

111.   8. The top number
minus the bottom left–hand
number multiplied by the
right–hand number.

112.   8. 3rd row - top row =
5th row. 5th row + 4th row =
2nd row.

113.   233
356
479
725
848
971

114.   Our answer is:

115.   217
366
515
664
813
962

116.   2 times.

117.   7. The top number
minus the bottom left–hand
number multiplied by the
right hand number.

118.   3. Top row + bottom
row = middle row.

119. 279
      441
      522
      846
      765
      927

120. Our answer is:

121. 122 (values of symbols ✪ = 20, ☆ = 24, ★ = 42, ☆ = 36).

122. In 2 ¼ years time. The outer planet is 22.5 degrees in its orbit, the sun is in the middle and the inner planet is at 202.5 degrees.

123.

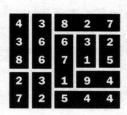

124. 2 ways.

125. 1, 3, and 4.

126. 126 at the side and 122 beneath (values of symbols: ☆ = 31, ✦ = 30, ✪ = 35).

127. 11 ways.

128.

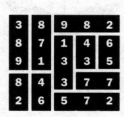

129. 58 and 37.

130. 6. The top number multiplied by the bottom left–hand number minus the right–hand number.

131.　5. The top row plus the second row gives the third row. The second row plus the fourth gives the fifth row.

132.　145
224
461
777
856
935

133.　Our answer is:

134.　53 (values of symbols: ☆ = 4, ✪ = 17, ✦ = 15).

135.　4 routes.

136.　6. 2nd row + 3rd row = top row. 3rd row + 4th row = 5th row.

137.　272
349
426
657
734
965

138.　Our answer is:

139.　148 (values of symbols: ✧ = 38, ☆ = 37, ✦ = 34).

140.　90 and 92.

141.

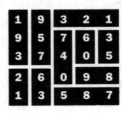

142.   4 ways.

143.   5. The top number is added to the bottom left–hand number and the bottom right–hand number is subtracted.

144.   3. The top row is the total of the 2nd and 3rd rows. The bottom row is the total of the 3rd and 4th rows.

145.   4 ½. The top number multiplied by the bottom left–hand number divided by the bottom right–hand number.

146   5U on the second row from the bottom.

147.

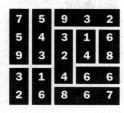

148.   54.

149.   4. The top number minus the two bottom numbers combined.

150.   2. The top row minus the bottom row gives the third row. The third row plus the second row gives the fourth row.

151.   195
       415
       635
       745
       855
       965

152.   Our answer is:

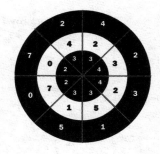

153.   47 (values of symbols ◈ = 6, ★ = 11, ☆ = 12, ◆ = 18).

154.　2 ways.

155.

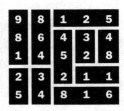

156　In twelve and a half years time. The outer planet is 45 degrees in its orbit, the sun is in the middle and the inner planet is at 225 degrees.

157.　6. A + B = D.
D − 3 = C. C + B = E.

158.　3U on the bottom row.

159.　34 ways.

160.　7, 8 and 15.

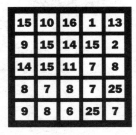

161.　Once.

162.　2 ways.

163.　5 spades.

164.　9 ways.

165.　8. A − B + 1 = D.
D − 1 = C.
B + C = E.

166.　3D on the top row.

167.　1. A + B − 1 = D.
D − 3 = C.
B + C = E

168.

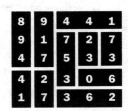

169. 10 clubs.

170.　7 ways.

171.   7. A + B = D.
       D − 3 = C.
       C + B = E.

172.   3R in the third column
from the left on the third
row down.

173.   7 ways.

174.   8, 12, 13 and 14.

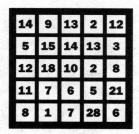

175.   19 ways.

176.   4 times.

177.   37 ways.

178.   9 ways.

179.   5, 8 and 11.

12	3	12	3	10
6	10	11	11	2
11	14	8	2	5
5	5	5	6	19
6	8	4	18	4

180.   8 times.

181.   6 times.

182.   9 clubs.

183.   7 ways.

184.   2. A − B = D.
       D + 2 = C.
       D − B = E

185.   2R on the third row
down in the fourth column
from the left.

186.   59 ways.

187.   3, 4 and 6.

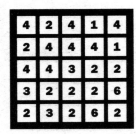

4	2	4	1	4
2	4	4	4	1
4	4	3	2	2
3	2	2	2	6
2	3	2	6	2

188.   13 ways.

189.   7. A – B = C.
C + 1 = D.
B + C = E.

190.   4U on the third row from the bottom.

191.   21 ways.

192.   15, 17 and 24.

17	4	17	5	17
4	17	17	17	5
17	17	12	7	7
15	7	7	7	24
7	15	7	24	7

193.   8 times.

194.   Once.

195.   3 diamonds.

196.   7 ways.

197.   7 clubs.

198.   9. A + B = D.
D – 3 = C.
C + B = E..

199.   Once.

200.   15.

201.   5 spades

202.   4 ways.